GODLY
Materialism

Rethinking Money & Possessions

JOHN SCHNEIDER

INTERVARSITY PRESS
DOWNERS GROVE, ILLINOIS 60515

*This book is dedicated to my wife, Winona,
and to my sons, Sol and Tom.*

*InterVarsity Press® is the book-publishing division of InterVarsity Christian Fellowship®, a student
movement active on campus at hundreds of universities, colleges and schools of nursing in the United States
of America, and a member movement of the International Fellowship of Evangelical Students. For information about local and regional activities, write Public Relations Dept., InterVarsity Christian Fellowship, 6400
Schroeder Rd., P.O. Box 7895, Madison, WI 53707-7895.*

*Scripture quotations, unless otherwise noted, are from the New Revised Standard Version of the Bible, copy-
right 1989 by the Division of Christian Education of the National Council of the Churches of Christ in the
U.S.A., and are used by permission.*

ISBN 0-8308-1667-4
Printed in the United States of America ∞

Library of Congress Cataloging-in-Publication Data

Schneider, John, 1951-
　　*Godly materialism: rethinking money and possessions/John
Schneider.*
　　　　p.　cm.
　　Includes bibliographical references.
　　ISBN 0-8308-1667-4
　　1. Wealth—Religious aspects—Christianity.　I. Title.
BR115.W4S36　1994
241'.68—dc20
　　　　　　　　　　　　　　　　　　94-411
　　　　　　　　　　　　　　　　　　CIP

17	16	15	14	13	12	11	10	9	8	7	6	5	4	3	2	1
08	07	06	05	04	03	02	01	00	99	98	97	96	95	94		

Preface

Most books come to life well before they are written, usually through a disturbance of the spirit. I think this one was conceived in 1973, when my wife took a job at World Vision International. For some time our daily exposure to world hunger through that organization made good food leave a bad taste in our mouths. In later years desire for an integrated Christian economic life took shape as a course, titled "A Theology of Wealth and Possessions," which I cotaught with Terry Eves at Westmont College. I should say here that I owe many of my first intuitions about the Old Testament and economic life to him. Although I no longer teach there, I must also express my indebtedness to Westmont College for supporting such an experimental course. Eventually my notes for the course began looking like the bare bones of a book. However, they lay at rest, interred in my files, until a sabbatical from Calvin College, my present employer, gave me the needed luxury of extended time to write it. I am most grateful to Calvin for its conviction that professional scholars are not the only ones who need to have books written for them. Indeed, had I written this book for the academic guild it would have included far more references to method and meaning (our collective obsession), and it would have been doubly thick with the requisite qualifications and tips of the hat to the experts in countless, specialized ghettos (and sometimes grottos) of expertise. I confess that I have been guilty of writing such books in the past, and no doubt will be again—but this is not one of them. I can but hope for a generous spirit from my colleagues, and that they may detect the mostly unstated theoretical work that stands behind this presentation to a less specialized but no less important readership.

The primary purpose of this book is to reach Christian people who have more than enough money but not enough sense of direction in their economic lives. I have aimed it at those Christians who take sacred Scripture as a source of truth in larger matters of faith and life. I know full well that my proposals often go against the grain of moral theology as it is commonly offered by our churches and centers of higher learning today. There is something in the book to offend just about everybody. My only request to the reader is for a critically open mind. The Lord knows that our culture is producing more than enough tiresome predictability through one or another version of "correctness" (on both on the right and the left). On that score, I will take my stand with the philosophers Socrates and Nietzsche, both of whom, in their quite different ways, were disdainful of what the latter liked to call the "bureaucracy of the mind." I for one will count this book a success if only it gets people thinking seriously about the core of their moral lives and provokes honest discussion and debate. If some of its ideas prove on examination to be false, then it will in that way have served those who have, by examining them, found greater truth and light.

1

THE IDENTITY
CRISIS
OF RICH
CHRISTIANS

The Lutherans also get a sermon about sacrifice, which the late Pastor Tommerdahl did so very well every year, entitling it "The True Meaning of Christmas," and if you went to the church with visions of sugarplums dancing in your head, he stopped the music. Santa Claus was not prominent in his theology. He had the gift of making you feel you'd better go home and give all the presents to the poor and spend Christmas with a bowl of soup, and not too many noodles in it either. He preached the straight gospel, and as he said, the gospel is meant to comfort the afflicted and afflict the comfortable. He certainly afflicted the Lutherans.

GARRISON KEILLOR, Lake Wobegon Days

I will never forget the student who appeared in my office one day. I was in my first year of teaching basic theology at an evangelical Christian college. The young man stood in the doorway for a moment and then lumbered into my office. He sat silently on the chair opposite mine. There was none of the usual student luster of brightness and innocence about him. I remember thinking that behind his effort to smile was a terrible sadness.

He had just come back from our "urban program," which allowed students to spend a semester living and working in San Francisco for college credit. Since our students came mostly from the upper middle class, they had never really been exposed firsthand to American urban problems. The experience was good for them, but it was hard. They almost always returned to our campus in a state of some alienation and distress. Their evangelical communities had not equipped them for anything like the suffering that they saw in the city. And so the students were themselves sorely afflicted by the afflictions of the world.

They were afflicted in different ways. Some went through a crisis of faith. They just could not comprehend how the God of evangelical love could permit the horrible suffering they had seen in the city. Some of them knew for the first time what Martin Luther called *Anfechtung,* a fiendish attack upon the simple, childlike soul. Faith would never again come to them without effort.

But the young man in my office was not having a crisis of faith. His exposure to suffering did not make him doubt God's existence or God's love for the world. He was instead having a crisis of identity, a crisis of self that is peculiar to certain rich Christians in our time. More exactly, it was an almost paralyzing crisis of guilt over who he was—a Christian with money and privilege in an age of suffering.

His guilt was exactly what Ronald Sider addressed (and confessed) in his influential book *Rich Christians in an Age of Hunger.*[1] His conscience had been stirred by what was for him a revolutionary new look at the biblical prophets. They had spoken against the rich on behalf of the poor and oppressed. Their God was a God who identified and sided with the poor in their struggle for freedom from the yoke of oppression. And their oppressors were the rich people of Israel. People like him.

The student had also discovered a very different Jesus from the gentle figure who inhabited the temples of his evangelical upbringing. This Jesus was radical in his identification with the poor, and to the rich he was a menacing figure. As one of the program speakers had put it, this Jesus had come to "comfort the afflicted and to afflict the comfortable."

All this was, indeed, quite new to the student, quite revolutionary and quite depressing. On top of all that, he had had his eyes opened to the evils of Western capitalism. He had learned that it was, in essence, a system *structured* for evil and immersed in evil, and he was of course immersed in it. No teaching, no word, could have been more alien to what he had learned his whole life; all that he had counted good, he now counted as a systemic expression of evil.

One of the most admired speakers on the urban program had suggested a way of repentance. He had told of a mother who was bursting with pride because her daughter had beaten out several hundred applicants for a teaching job in a good public school in the suburbs. The mother was so proud of her daughter's success that she went around beaming, telling all her friends. But wait just a minute, the speaker had urged. "Success?" Really? Why hadn't the daughter applied for one of those teaching jobs that nobody wants? Why hadn't she taken a job in a bad school where she was sorely needed by poor children? The proud mother and well-meaning daughter had unwittingly compromised the gospel, for they had conformed to the spirit of the world. The speaker exhorted the students to reject the worldly logic of "upward mobility" and to practice a truly Christlike "downward mobility." Other speakers and books advocated "simpler living" combined with fervent involvement in churches and in the political process toward social change. My student could only look with contempt on his previous plans to work in his father's marketing corporation and all that went with it. He felt his whole world coming apart. And yet, in the advice of his sages he found a counsel of despair, for he could not be other than what he was.

I was not sure what to say to him. Rather thinly, I did help him to understand one thing that I knew to be true and urgent for all Christians to know about their faith. That is, to be a Christian *is*, and always has been, to struggle for a right and good economic identity. What he had experienced was normal by historical standards. In fact, there was something quite *abnormal* about the absence of soul-searching and real conflict within his circle of evangelical Christians.

I believe he found some consolation in learning that Christians in almost every previous age understood that they must agonize over this question.[2] But what does it mean to live the Christian economic life with real integrity?

Moral Beliefs and Their Power

My student was finding out the hard way what his philosophy professors had taught him in lectures—that moral beliefs are powerful things. Our moral beliefs—our beliefs about what is good, evil or indifferent—shape our unconscious and conscious minds. These beliefs, along with our religious beliefs, make us the persons that we become in life. They are like maps that direct our way, or like rules of a game that dictate how we act in certain circumstances, or like lenses through which we "see" reality. All beliefs shape us in one way or another, but our moral beliefs are "person shaping" beliefs. My belief that it is raining shapes my perspective and even my actions—I may bring an umbrella to work or check the windshield wipers on my car before leaving. But my *moral* beliefs shape my life, my identity as a person and my responses to other persons. My student's beliefs about the morality of economic life in America would shape his whole identity and life.

False moral beliefs thus often lead to great harm and wrongdoing. The Roman soldiers who crucified Jesus apparently *believed* that they were doing the right thing. But unwittingly they committed an unspeakable evil. People can also believe that something is evil when it is not. It may even be good. This also leads to confusion and wrongdoing. A local pastor was seen drinking at a cocktail party. Because some of his congregation believed that the consumption of alcohol was morally wrong, especially for a pastor, they judged him unfit for the ministry. It did no good to explain to them that the pastor was making ties with local politicians to get a badly needed orphanage built in town. And they simply would not hear the biblical case for affirming the proper use of wine and spirits.

Our beliefs about economic life are at bottom moral beliefs. We must therefore form them with utmost care, to the extent that we have control over them. We do not wish to believe that our economic life is good when it is really evil, as the student feared his was, for obviously that would be disastrous. We would be in the grotesque state of actually opposing Christ while claiming to be his followers. But there is another danger too. We also do not wish to engage in unhealthy or misdirected moral judgment and guilt. We do not wish to believe that our economic life is evil when it is in fact essentially good. In this case we would go around wrongly condemning ourselves and other good people as evildoers. Our posture would then be that of injustice in one of its most ironic and cruelest forms—moralizing judgmentalism. And we ourselves would become either painfully self-righteous and judgmental in just the manner Scripture strictly forbids, or we could become, like my despairing student who believed he could not really be otherwise, needlessly sick of soul.

There is little happiness, by the way, in the ending of my story about the student. In spite of his discoveries, he went off to work in his father's corporation. But he went in a state of surrender, resignation and guilt, because he still felt that what he was doing was sinful at bottom. He just could not bring himself to be anything other than what he was, the son of a middle-class corporate executive. It was a formula for failure, passive aggression and all sorts of things that cripple people psychologically every day, when they believe that they are being driven by larger forces to compromise and even prostitute themselves for gain.

Delight and the Big Chill

Regrettably, many Christian professionals suffer from unresolved moral conflict and guilt over their economic identities, and it affects every level of their lives. This book is written largely to them. I am writing particularly for people whom I have known through the years, people who are in various ways dear to me. They are mostly committed Christians who have stayed within the mainstream. They are working within the system, but they have lingering questions. They wonder if they have not compromised something very important. They wonder deep down if their work and lifestyle comport with Christian faith. They have a lingering sense that they are guilty of something. They are children of a kind of Christian "Big Chill" (referring to the film about university graduates who had been great idealists and social activists in the sixties but had become successful members of the establishment). I am thinking of countless men and women, many of them good friends of mine. They are successful professionals—doctors, lawyers, business people, writers, corporate executives, engineers, investors, educators and so forth. They are women and men of considerable intelligence and drive. They set a high standard for themselves and others. They are (or are on the way toward becoming) financially secure, if not extremely rich, and most adopt a lifestyle that is more or less commensurate with that of the middle or upper middle classes. Their identities are rooted in this cultural system that one may call "the American Way."

These Christians strongly believe that there is something right and good about living an abundant life. They feel that there is something right about a system that encourages and liberates people to work hard, to be productive, and to pursue their dreams. They believe that there is something right and good about safe neighborhoods and solid schools for their children. They believe that there is something right about having a secure house and home. They sense that it is good to enjoy not just the "necessaries" of life, as Charles Wesley put it, but the "delights" of being human.

And if you think about it, most human "delight" is connected with physical experience. The delights of sex, aesthetic beauty, fine food and drink, handsome clothing, finely built and well-tuned cars, wondrous video and sound systems—all such delights are essentially physical. Our natural delight in certain material possessions (which are pure luxuries by any meaningful standard) is deeply connected with the native power of the physical world to "delight" us, and in our human capacity to be delighted by it. And our American culture has taught us to believe that this delight is *good*. Not only is it good, we think, but it is an expression of our human dignity, essential to "the good life."

But is this really true? For many reflective Christians, delight is always hollowed at the center by the powers of guilt. Such people often live with deep moral tension, although it may not come conspicuously to the surface.

The people I have in mind are sensitive to the problems of domestic poverty and world hunger. They know the statistical truism that the United States consumes an immense portion of the world's resources. They know the standard criticisms of the wealthy nations and their economic abuses. They have stared into the blank eyes of hungry children on cable television and heard the cries of desperate mothers in Dolby stereo who come into their homes, as by some mythical magic, across the airwaves. They read the papers, and when they read about the Catholic bishops' letter (1985) that condemned evils in the capitalistic systems of the West, they feel twinges of personal guilt and wonder about their own lives.

The other evening I sat on my newly built cedar deck. I looked around at the giant oaks standing surrounding the house. I watched as my children played innocently and safely in a landscape that has become to them a wonder-filled world of projects and endless fantasies. As I enjoyed the smells and tastes of the summer barbecue I was moved to feel sheer gratitude to God and to those before me who made this life possible. I was overwhelmed with the thought that life is indeed good, a gift from God. But then I thought, can it be true that this "suburban" identity of mine is badly wrong and that in some deep sense my evening and all the delights connected with it were really "sinful" in God's eyes? How could that be? I thought. But many of us feel somewhere deep down that we are failing as Christians—precisely because of our suburban (or wealthy urban) existence. Do we not suspect that we are somehow inferior for enjoying so many "delights" in a hungry world? Is this not the ungodly materialism that all Christians must condemn? Or is it?

The literature today, from leaders in both the church and the academy, is sharply polarized on this question. The life of material delight that we associate with our middle and upper classes is often pitted directly against the life of radical social and economic compassion. Or it goes the other way: the life of justice is incompatible with a life of comparative enjoyment. On one side, usually in the popular evangelical camp, the Bible is treated almost like a divinely inspired annuity brochure for successful American Christians. But on the other side, usually the more academic, an unwitting observer might conclude that sacred Scripture was written as a handbook for modern social (socialistic) revolution.

Why the difference between people of the same faith reading and using the same book? The conflict drives deeply into the nature of Scripture itself. Anyone can see that the Bible contains texts that affirm material prosperity as God's blessing and that it also contains texts that condemn riches as a curse. As with many profound theological questions, there is no ready-made and obvious way of affirming *all* of Scripture as giving forth a single, coherent vision of economic life for God's people. Some would even say such a vision is impossible. I disagree. But we must work hard to find the unity of God's Word within its diverse voices.

The question then is, Is there a kind of delight that also embraces justice? Is true godliness possible for people like us who enjoy the good things of life in a world of hunger? Or to put it bluntly, is there such a thing as a "godly materialism"? If the answer to that question seems immediately obvious—one way or the other—then I do not think we have quite grasped the profundity of the problem.

I do believe that, in the end, Scripture does not pit material delight against the radical pursuit of social justice, as is done with few exceptions in the literature of today. In fact (so I believe), it envisions the two as deeply and delicately interconnected. They both turn out to be expressions of the redeemed and redeeming life before God. It even seems that the one cannot rightly exist without the other. There is no true prosperity or delight without compassion and justice; but likewise, there is no real justice or liberation, no *shalom*, without material delight and flourishing.

I have come to believe, then, that there is a godly way of living the life of material delight—a "godly materialism"—just as there is obviously an ungodly one. Showing from the many texts of Scripture that this is so is no simple task. Nevertheless, that is the main goal and purpose of this book.

I sincerely hope that my primary readers, Christians with more than enough money, will find in the book both the burden of moral challenge and the lightness of personal liberation. It was the divine and human genius of our Lord, Jesus, that he laid the heaviest of obligations on his people while at the same time setting them free, enlarging and empowering them to be the persons God created them to be. His "yoke" was indeed a yoke, but it was strangely light.

Jesus did indeed identify himself with the economic poor, but, if we are attuned to it, there was also in his great personhood a powerful moment of identification with the rich, and thus with us. But it is no easy thing to grasp, or to live out, that moment in the right way. In the spirit of such demanding compassion, this book seeks to bring a word of liberation to Christians whom God has enriched with wealth.

2

CHRISTIANS & MONEY THROUGH THE CENTURIES

A people without a history is like the wind on the buffalo grass.
AMOS BAD HEART BULL, Lakota Sioux historian

W ithout understanding the past, we are unable to understand ourselves," wrote church historian Justo Gonzalez.[1] Indeed, nothing is comprehensible apart from its past. And it is certainly true that today's church is in dire need of greater historical literacy. Christianity is the product of nearly two thousand years of development through time. Simply studying the Bible, as is often done, without knowing the interpretations (tradition), trials and errors of centuries gone dooms Christians to repeat the mistakes of the past—without knowing it—or naively to invent brand-new ones. Someone once compared studying history to walking through a vast field of tall grass. When we lose our sense of direction, we instinctively find a hill and look back to see the trail we have left behind. The trampled line helps us again to know the east from the west, so that we may move purposefully onward.

History gives depth of perspective and a sense of direction. But unfortunately, it is not an infallible guide. Even the great ones among the ancients were more immersed in and infected by their cultures than they knew. While they made progress in understanding the faith, they would be the first to admit that, as vessels of truth, they were imperfect. And of course their times were not exactly the same as ours. They could not address their brilliance to the questions that our age of science, technology, industry and commerce has generated for Christians. The economic world that we are called to be "in" but not "of" is unlike anything they could even vaguely imagine. But these giants, on whose shoulders we do stand, can help us to see the deeper vision of being a Christian in the world, for the deeper truths of God's Word have not changed and the world is spiritually the same as it has always been.

What follows here is only a survey of historic Christian approaches to economic life. Professional historians will recognize immediately that this is no complete scholarly account, and it does not pretend to be one. It is instead what I believe to be a useful typology, a look at the main "types" of Christian economic identity that have emerged in times past. The purpose is to help us to see what the ablest minds of the church have deemed the most plausible interpretations of Scripture in their varying times and circumstances.

Recent studies prove that the matter of "mammon" was at the core of Christian theology and life from the very beginning of the church.[2] What made this such an urgent concern was the record of Jesus' own radical life and teachings in the Gospels, and also Luke's startling picture of economic life among the first Christians in the book of Acts. It seems that the New Testament put the whole Jewish, Greek and Roman economic culture under an intense scrutiny. The budding Christian faith did not just assimilate to itself the standard cultural assumptions about acquiring, enjoying and using wealth. Nor did it permit itself simply to be assimilated by the surrounding economic culture. By its very nature, the new gospel of Jesus forced believers to distance themselves from accepted economic habits and norms. Rather than allowing them to "go with the flow" of economic life, it demanded that they reflect on it and that they move against the stream. Christians disagreed on finer points of just which currents to resist, but it is no exaggeration to say that all those who wrote on the subject understood these questions to be an intense inquiry into the matter of spiritual life, a matter of salvation itself.

The questions were fresh, the possibilities many, the answers sometimes various, especially at first. Should they separate themselves from the world of trade and commerce? Or should they work *in* the world? If not, what then? But if so, how could they avoid being *of* that world, compromising the integrity of their faith? A crucial issue was what seemed a radical challenge to property rights in Scripture—rights that Roman law and culture presumed to be absolute. Christians wondered, should they divest themselves of all capital and property? Some read the New Testament to teach as much. Others disagreed. But, again, if owning property was allowed, then it was not at all obvious what the moral conditions for this might be. When was ownership good rather than evil? How was one to think Christianly about the whole concept of owning? It reveals much about the character of early Christianity and its Scriptures that the defenders of private property, rather than its opponents, had the heavier burden of proof on them in the debate. It is very important to know that the eventual affirmation of private property was not as obvious to the early church as it is to many Christians today. This perhaps teaches us something about ourselves, too, that we would rather not hear.

Connected with *owning* was the question of the right means of *acquiring* wealth. Assuming that ownership was sometimes good, theologians wondered whether wealth could rightly come only by heredity, or whether Christians might acquire it through purposeful enterprise in commercial trade or in some other form of business. We see that the gospel forced very basic questions; it drove Christians back to ponder their very first principles. Things were complicated by concerns about moneylending, which the Bible seemed clearly to forbid. And there was an added distinction between the typical form of business, which was agriculture (90 percent of the economy then), and what seemed to many the more questionable way of making money through commercial businesses.

For most thinkers, the question boiled down to the issue of the right spiritual and moral modes of having. What counted in the end was a spirituality of love in the context of wealth. At very least that meant that the Christian's economic identity and life were shaped by love of God and neighbor and not by the love of money. She, or he, must at all costs avoid a spiritual disposition of *greed* and, in expression of godliness and love, must put wealth to really good *use*. Early Christians usually thought of this as some form of charity, especially toward the poor.

Could wealth also be enjoyed in the luxury of excess? It seems that most early Christian thinkers were quite skeptical that it might be so. Whether we adopt their final judgments or not, we shall be wise not to ignore their deepened conscience of skepticism toward extravagance.

So we see that debates about money, on just about every level of the subject, are nothing new among Christians. We must understand, as did they, that the whole matter of economic identity is a matter of Christian identity. It cannot be otherwise for a faith that refuses to separate body from spirit, works from faith, and God and the world. In this we can learn much about true spirituality—the ancients knew what many rich Christians today must learn to know. Followers of Jesus Christ simply may not live like pagans in the marketplace while claiming to be Christians in church.

In this chapter I have sketched three "types" of Christian teaching on economic life that have arisen in church history.[3] I have given references to larger historical works where the interested reader may find more thorough and nuanced treatments. No doubt other models could be given. Nevertheless, I think that these three "types" generally constitute the main options, the syntheses that have been available and viable to most Christians through the years and that have the most relevance to most rich Christians today.

I have named and presented the "types" in the order of their historical appearance: "Historic Catholicism," "Historic Protestantism" and "New World Theology." As the name states, the first is typical of traditional Catholic theology before its collision with modernity. The great St. Augustine played a large role in establishing this model, and he will be my primary example of it. The typical Protestant pattern is found in the writings of Martin Luther and John Calvin. Safe to say, these views (the Catholic and Protestant) were the dominant models in Europe until the opening of the New World, which brought unimagined changes in society. Both of the Old World visions affirmed the basic goodness of the material world and (by extension) the goodness of owning and using material property to serve in the kingdom of God, especially with respect to helping the poor through charity. There were deep differences, especially over the issue of monastic life and its value. Still, I believe that Catholics and Protestants were more in agreement on economic issues than not. Both affirmed the goodness of creation, that it was good to work, to acquire and to own property under conditions of right use. Both traditions imagined right use in terms of self-sacrifice on behalf of others, particularly the really poor and powerless. And both great European traditions were deeply suspicious of extravagance. For both, reform was almost synonymous with attack on material self-gratification in the church.

Finally, both Catholic and Protestant intellectuals were ill-prepared for the shock of the New World economic and cultural order. That is because neither tradition could foresee a world beyond the great revolutions—democratic, scientific and industrial—that would make life in the Middle Ages a distant memory. They did not envision whole nations with cultures defined by these revolutions. Luther and Calvin have often been painted as forerunners of the modern capitalist mind and of the spirit of Christian capitalism, and this picture is to an extent true. But their writings show that they were themselves spiritually troubled by what they knew of the emerging mercantile system and the values of the middle class growing in Europe.

Profound and powerful social forces simply changed the Christian economic imagination, including its theology and spirituality regarding the creation, enjoyment and use of material wealth. The birth of the New World was literally the death of older assumptions about what the economic world was—that which Christians must somehow be "in" but not "of." As we shall see, ancient economic systems had failed to create freedom and wealth for very many people. On the contrary, they were systems of the "top-down" variety, driven by autocracy and profitable only to a few. Wealth flowed toward the top, and poverty was the normal state of existence for the vast majority. Until the Industrial Revolution and afterward, this was generally accepted as a fact of life in Christian theology. It was as Jesus had said: "The poor you will always have with you." The idea of actually *eliminating* poverty, rather than just nursing away some of its effects (through almsgiving and the like), is something quite recent to the Christian mind.

So also is our idea of "the good life" as one of material fruitfulness and abundance. However we judge the morality of the matter, it is important to understand that the new social order of democracy and capitalism gave quite ordinary people unimagined freedom to attain a quite extraordinary level of wealth and, thus, control over their lives.[4] No wonder Christians in early America became so optimistic about possibilities on *this* side of the grave that they came to see in the structures of culture a more-than-human experiment in the making.[5]

My main interest (in this chapter and through the book) is in the deeper, timeless theological vision that *shapes* and controls our expressed beliefs and judgments about economic identity and life in one era or another. These are interconnected depth-beliefs about what was, what is and what ought to be the right spiritual and moral order on earth. We might call it the depth-structure of the Christian consciousness, mind or imagination, the picture of sacred reality that comes before and shapes our attitudes, beliefs and actions in response to one economic system or another. For the Christian, this is primarily a matter of comprehending the worldview that underlies and comes with the Christian gospel. And for orthodox Christians, this is first a matter of reading and interpreting Scripture. Obviously we cannot be other than products of our own social and economic circumstances, but we can seek to place this reading and interpreting of God's Word first, so that we may begin, if only "through a glass darkly," to see and to judge our culture with eyes and hearts not merely our own. With God's help, and the accumulated wisdom of the ages, we may see the world, in its spiritual and moral dimensions, more clearly for what it is. And thus we may begin to see ourselves more clearly for what we are, and for what we (and it) ought to be, in this troubled time of ours. To the ages we thus now turn.

Historic Catholicism: The Saint and the World

In the first two centuries of the church, a good number of Christians tried to separate themselves almost completely from the world. They withdrew from the marketplace, got rid of their possessions and headed for the deserts. Their motivation to separate from the world was not based on the same ideas of reality, however. Some of these people were motivated by belief that the material world was itself evil. The most extreme end of this movement (fairly widespread in the early second century) is often labeled Gnosticism.[6] Church authorities judged Gnostics and their assault on the creation as deeply pagan, not at all Christian. The earliest creed of the emerging orthodox church, the Apostles' Creed, began, "I believe in God the Father Almighty, maker of heaven and earth." In this one statement, the essence of Gnosticism was defeated, the essential *goodness* of the material world redeemed. The goodness of the material world has not been in serious debate among professing Christians since that time. The debate on economic life has presumed the goodness of creation, the essential goodness of the physical body and of material things, and has centered on other things, related to the cluster of questions described above.

The theology of the great St. Augustine (A.D. 354-430) helps to make the categories of the early Christian debate clear, and it also shows the way chosen by mainstream Catholic tradition. The issue of material wealth had always burned among Christians. But it came to a head at the beginning of the fourth century when the emperor Constantine made Christianity legal and established it as the dominant religion of the culture.[7] Christianity had been illegal until then, and Christians were used to being treated badly by the state. Sometimes they were mercilessly persecuted by the authorities. At best they suffered in subtle ways that kept them on the margins of social power. But under Constantine, who had experienced something of a conversion to Christianity, the church entered into a strange new moral situation. Christianity made a meteoric rise to the heights of prestige and influence in the world's most powerful civilization. Suddenly many of the rich and powerful families of Rome converted to the faith. Huge church buildings grew in every major city, and great pomp and circumstance attended public worship. Jesus' little "mustard seed" had indeed grown into the greatest of trees. Christianity became the "civil religion" of Rome.[8]

Not everyone found in this cause to celebrate. Some Christians wore their suffering as a badge of honor, and they reacted strongly against the new situation of harmony with the state. They resented it that becoming a Christian was now "the thing to do." They found it loathsome that a spirit of Roman triumphalism had replaced the militant, long-suffering theology of the cross that had for so long defined the faith. Like today, some rigorous Christians did not think that worldly success and Christian faith could well occur together. They feared that the church might indeed gain the whole world but, by failing to carry its cross, lose its soul.

In reaction, the older monastic movement grew stronger, producing a very important Christian counterpoint to the cultural religion. Some argued that separation from the world was required;[9] others argued the opposite, claiming that it was possible to remain faithful *in* the world.[10] Some inveighed against having property at all, although most agreed that work and ownership of property in some form was essential simply to the biblical vision of caring for the body and for others in serving God.

But there was strong support, in contrast to Roman culture, for the idea of communal ownership, sharing the common wealth that God had given to the earth.[11] This ideal, however, constantly fell to the realities of life in a fallen world.[12] This meant that for many Christians, living in the world with property was an option of the "second best" variety, a concession to sin more than a celebration of life, liberty and property in Christian form. The unreality of communism was indeed apparent even then to wise minds, but this hardly generated enthusiasm for anything like our ideals of capitalism.

By Augustine's time, it was necessary to provide a Christian rationale for the inevitable ownership of things by individuals and families. Finally, it seems that all Christian writers condemned the superfluous, the enjoyment of "more than was needed," and pressed for charity based on meeting the needs of other human beings, and so especially the poor.[13]

Augustine forged (as he did on so many issues) the answer that became the framework for the mainstream Christian view for centuries to come. He reaffirmed the Christian view that the creation is good, and so thus are the body, material things and the right sort of relationship between them. They are good in a religious, sacred sense. Material things are instances of God's good world. Thus, he rejected the counsel of required separation from the culture and supported a model of Christian engagement. (We will see below, however, that for Augustine as well as for historic Catholicism, engagement was still "second best" in important respects.)

Augustine made two important distinctions that enabled him to develop his theory of ownership and Christian economic life in the world. First he drew a line between material things themselves and the *possession* of those things.[14] The reality of wood and stone is itself good, but to have them as *wealth*—as our own *house*, say—is a very different matter. He did, it should be added, affirm the right to private property and the acquisition of wealth through all the legal cultural means—agriculture, trade and/or commerce.[15] But whether or not it is good to have land, or a house, or money, and to work productively with such capital, is not settled by their intrinsic goodness. The goodness of acquiring and having "goods" is decided rather by spiritual and moral conditions. Like most theologians before him, he argued that it is settled by how we acquire our possessions and by how we hold and use them after we acquire them. "Greed is not a defect in the gold that is desired, but in the man who loves it perversely by falling from justice."[16] Going back to our modern example, owning a home might be good, in Augustine's system, but it might not be. The moral status of ownership would depend on the conditions that defined the morality of our having. Augustine connected these conditions both with our intent (unhealthy desire) and with our social actions (injustice). Goods must be acquired without covetousness, and justly.

But what exactly were the conditions suggested by Augustine's reference to greed and injustice? Could luxuries like grilled steaks and fine wine also be good, or are such delights off limits? To define his conditions more precisely, Augustine made the distinction that has since become classically associated with his name. He marked a sharp line between *enjoyment* and *use.* In now-famous words, he wrote: "Some things are to be enjoyed, others are to be used, and there are others which are to be enjoyed and used."[17] By "enjoyment" *(fruitio)*, Augustine meant "to cling to it with love for its own sake."[18] On the other hand, to put something to "use" *(usus)* was "to employ it in obtaining that which you love, provided it is worthy of love."[19]

To illustrate, Augustine asked us to imagine traveling to our homeland: "We would need vehicles for land and sea which could be used to help us reach our homeland, which is to be enjoyed."[20] But if we fell in love with the vehicles and the journey itself, taking delight in them for their own sake, we should become "entangled in a perverse sweetness, we should be alienated from our country, whose sweetness would make us blessed."[21] Augustine concluded by offering this as a metaphor for our life of "traveling" through the world: "Thus in this mortal life, wandering from God, if we wish to return to our native country where we can be blessed *we should use this world and not enjoy it.*"[22] Notice that even though in his parable he seems to count our earthly homeland as something to be "enjoyed," his explicit point is that "corporal and temporal things" are not to be "enjoyed" but "used" for a higher purpose, that "we may comprehend the eternal and spiritual."[23] Clearly, God, as Father, Son and Spirit, is to be "enjoyed," whereas the things of the world are essentially to be "used" and thus not loved for their own sake. Worldly goods are truly "goods" only insofar as they serve as vehicles for getting us to our eternal homeland. The answer to our question about luxuries is becoming clear; they would seem to qualify as "enjoyment" of the world, rather than as "use" in its right form.

Obviously, Augustine put simple, unqualified delight into serious moral question. His illustration pictures it as sweet seduction from the way toward heaven. It is widely known that in his teachings, physically pleasurable experiences with sex, food, drink and other worldly sources of delight were vigorously brought into connection with their right, instrumental uses—sex with procreation, food and drink with sustaining the body, all to the end of contemplating and enjoying God. The pleasures associated with these actions were for him more indicators of fixation on the world than they were gifts from God to be enjoyed. Thus we are to moderate or even repress them to the extent that we can. The same applies to material wealth and possessions.

With this distinction between "enjoyment" and "use," Augustine thus approved of living in the world and working for the acquisition and use of material wealth and possessions of various kinds, primarily to meet our own physical needs. But the goodness of having "goods" lies not therein, that we delight in the things themselves, only rather in the enjoyment of God that this use of things makes possible. They are mere instruments with which to reach the desired end. We can be said rightly to enjoy them only insofar as they are taken up in the larger act of enjoying God.

It is hardly surprising, then, that Augustine, in defining right use, follows the consensus of earlier Christian thinkers and draws a bold line between our material *needs* and our merely superfluous *wants*. This pattern of reasoning has had a powerful influence on the Christian spirit for centuries. And it is making something of a comeback among Christians today. Like most before him, Augustine judged that once our basic needs were met, our eyes must turn, out of love, away from ourselves toward respect for the dignity of others, especially the poor. Our own consumption of superfluous wealth could only amount to "enjoyment" and thus to abuse. He preached that "not to give to those in want what is superfluous is akin to fraud."[24] He summed up his view on the matter: "From those things that God gave you, take that which you need, but the rest, which to you are superfluous, are necessary to others. The superflous goods of the rich are necessary to the poor, *and when you possess the superfluous you possess what is not yours.* "[25] When we give alms to the poor, we store up treasure for ourselves in heaven, as Jesus commanded.[26]

Conceding that human hearts are hardened to this radical command, he counseled that the rich at least set aside one tenth of their superfluous wealth as a minimal gesture of good faith.[27] But this was a concession to, not an affirmation of, delight. Delight in the superfluous was, nonetheless, "enjoyment," as sinful as it was commonplace, a sign of weakness rather than of real success and blessedness among Christians in a hungry world. Augustine thus helped to develop the broad outline of a moral framework that philosophers today call "utilitarianism," because of its stress on social utility in meeting the greatest needs and its moral condemnation of enjoying luxuries while others are poor. By typical American standards, Augustine's model of the Christian economic life paints an austere picture. Having a house, food and drink may be to have "goods," but only in the context of meeting basic needs in love. Some today wish to revive this early Christian utilitarianism as a truly biblical model. Of this revival, much more later in the book.

We must also look quickly at one last area of Augustine's economic vision, his counsel of monasticism. Augustine developed strict conditions for Christians living in the mainstream of society. But rather than pit life in the world against monasticism, and vice versa, as had often been done, he wished to affirm the virtues of both by ordering them as lower and higher goods.[28] Here he offered another distinction, this time between moral obligations (what all Christians were required to do) and acts of *supererogation*. Such acts were not required by biblical law, but they were deemed good. To perform them was to "go the second mile," to act "above and beyond the call of duty." Many of Christ's radical teachings, such as in the Sermon on the Mount, were classified this way by earlier and later Catholic thinkers. This allowed them to take the Lord's life seriously as a model without also condemning the lives of those who remained in the culture. As for wealth, Augustine reasoned that Christ did not *require* Christians to imitate him and thus to live in poverty, but he did teach that *freely* to adopt such a life was virtuous, more virtuous in fact than life in the culture. To adopt such a life was an act of supererogation that improved our moral standing before God. It contributed to spiritual perfection and sainthood in this life. This premise became widely held in the church throughout the Middle Ages: living and working in the everyday world was good (having satisfied the proper moral conditions), but monastic life, with its vow of poverty and its communal ownership of goods, while not for everyone, was better.[29]

In sum, Augustine helped to establish what we may call the three main pillars of Catholic Christian tradition on economic life.[30] First, Catholic theology established this basic cluster of affirmations: the goodness of the creation, the God-given dignity of work (including in the commercial world), productivity and the possession of property (even in individual form). This pillar has only rarely been challenged in the history of the church, but is under severe scrutiny today, for there has been increased interest in communism among twentieth-century theologians.[31] The second pillar is the establishment of "utilitarian" moral reasoning about the use and enjoyment of wealth by persons working in the world. For them the ideal prescribes a model of "meeting need" rather than one that affirms "enjoyment and delight" as part of the Christian life-vision. The third pillar is the elevation of poverty to a higher station than being relatively rich. The doctrine of supererogation actually says that ordinary life is good but, in view of Christ's radically impoverished life, the monastic life is better, ideal in fact. On this last point Protestantism would make wrenching and important changes. But I believe it remained basically in line with the intuitions expressed by the first two pillars.

New World theology would one day force a radical reexamination of the second pillar, the utilitarian principle. I believe that this second pillar is at the center of today's most intense debate for North American professionals. The first and third pillars are not as central, although an anticommercialism, with respect to the first, has returned to certain sectors of the church, and there is a certain monastic spirit, if not theology, behind the revival of utilitarianism.

Historic Protestantism: The Worldly Saint

In the sixteenth century the Protestant Reformation brought about some fresh ways of thinking on economic life. One widespread view is that European Protestantism differed greatly from Catholicism by promoting a more worldly mentality and by fastening itself to early capitalism. Some have even argued that modern capitalism is "Protestantism without God."[32]

There were indeed differences between these two great versions of the Christian faith. Perhaps the most glaring one was the Protestant attack on monasticism and its vow of poverty. Martin Luther (1483-1546), John Calvin (1509-1564) and other Reformers indeed denied that the monastic life was morally superior to life in the world.[33] They came to believe that monasticism was in essence a desperate effort to whip oneself into shape before God, which was impossible. God meets us where we are—in butcher shops, chicken yards, vineyards, laundry rooms. Except in the case of immoral occupations like prostitution or thievery, God does not call us away from our secular work to a separate arena of spiritual athleticism. Engagement was not "second-best," it was itself the sacred calling of the saints. God calls us to faith in our endlessly different circumstances. The Reformers pointed out that the New Testament labels all faithful people "saints." Indeed, their experience with the monastaries led the Reformers to think that monastic life was high-level religious escapism. They often wrote of it as morally inferior to our everyday struggle in the marketplace of the "real world." They frowned on the whole idea of "supererrogation" and self-perfection through extraordinary works of merit. Their critique of monasticism vastly broadened the scope of what counted as a *religious* vocation for Christians. And it led eventually to a more "worldly" idea of "sainthood."

While this side of Protestantism added a kind of force to the spirit of modern capitalism, the original sources prove that European Protestantism was deeply imprinted by Catholicism. On basic issues, they remained more or less in agreement. Both mainstream Catholics and Protestants upheld private property for similar reasons. Moreover, in their reforming moments, both tended to define "reform" over and against worldliness and materialism. The major Protestant figures were very close to the utilitarian mindset of Augustine and Thomas Aquinas. And both traditions were deeply suspicious of the new banking system, the rising middle class and its way of life. Bourgeois capitalism as we know it was only just getting started.

The major Protestants affirmed the principle of proper *use* in somewhat the same terms as Augustine did, although without quite the same strict division between use and enjoyment. Luther was famous for his capacity to enjoy good German beer, food and table fellowship. But he was deeply offended by signs of self-indulgence among the nobility and also by the emerging middle class of merchants, investors and bankers, not only for their loaning at interest. Whatever his capacity to enjoy life, Luther had no feeling for the growing spirit of acquisition that he detected. As banking systems and a whole mercantile class began to emerge, he intensified the Catholic condemnation of "usury." In Luther we hear echoes of earlier theologians of the land: it would be better for people to go back to the land, where God intended them to live and work.[34] So we should not take Luther's worldliness on vocation and his fresh biblical approval of mundane delight in food, drink, sex and other created pleasures as clearly affirming anything like the spirit of our modern bourgeois life.[35]

John Calvin, likewise, wrote (on the basis of Scripture) that "we have never been forbidden to laugh, or to be filled, or to join new possessions to old ancestral ones, or to delight in musical harmony, or to drink wine."[36] But not to be "forbidden" to do something is hardly to accentuate it as a great good. And indeed (as many studies have shown) this is not the direction in which his thought developed. In contrast to some later Calvinists who took abundance simply as a blessing from God, Calvin's writings are filled with the language of moderation and sober self-denial. He even wrote that self-denial was "the sum of the Christian life."[37] The faithful life was a matter of "soberness, righteousness and godliness." By "soberness" Calvin meant "chastity and temperance as well as a pure and frugal use of temporal goods."[38] In very traditional (Catholic) terms, he wrote that we must devote temporal goods both to God and to the common good. And using the keyword of stewardship, he judged that the "rule for our generosity and beneficence" is "that we are stewards of everything God has conferred on us by which we are able to help our neighbor. . . . Moreover, the only right stewardship is that which is tested by the rule of love."[39]

Calvin approved of "delight" in goods inherited from our ancestors, and he blessed the use and enjoyment of music and wine. Still, his greater counsel came in a spirit of stern moderation, self-sacrifice and charity. His logic often verged on the utilitarian, and thus he opposed the luxurious. Food was more for the body, so he wrote, than it was something to bring enjoyment to the heart. In his words, "God nourishes them [Christians] to live, not to luxuriate."[40]

Although they gave Christians greater scope for worldly work and (perhaps) the enjoyment of worldly things, it is hard to imagine Luther or Calvin having much good to say about our consumption-driven, credit-powered systems and lifestyles. Even granting the anachronistic nature of the example, I cannot picture Calvin speeding along the freeway in a BMW (or even a Chevrolet) making appointments on his car phone. It might be somewhat easier to picture Luther grilling steaks on a backyard deck, or listening to music (probably Bach) on a good CD player, but the new world of capital, free markets, big business, international trade and investment was but a dim light on the Reformers' horizon. And what they saw of it did not make them glad or hopeful about the future. We shall not make a smooth transition into the modern world using only their ideas.

Protestantism (to risk very broad generalization), then, maintained two of the three main "pillars" of Catholic thought. It preserved the basic teaching of Catholic tradition on the goodness of the world and the individual's dignity and right to own property. And although it opened the secular world of work and life to "saintliness," destroying some of its monastic instinct, mainstream Protestantism remained faithful to the counsel of austerity in love. It was decidedly hostile to the superfluous, and it was thus sensitive to immorality in the spirit of early capitalism at that point. We shall see how all that would change—for Protestants and Catholics alike—in the strange new world whose birth they only glimpsed.

New World Theology: The Godly Merchant

If you look on the back of any dollar bill you will find the Great American Seal. On it is the Latin phrase *Novus Ordo Seclorum,* "the new order of the ages." The seal heralds the birth of something new on the planet. The framers believed that America was not just a new nation, but a new *order* for all nations through the ages. The reordering of American institutions had a powerful effect on Christian thinking about wealth and property.[41]

Perhaps the most astonishing change was a powerful shift from use (in its classical sense) as the dominant concept for regulating economic life, to the language of enjoyment and blessing from God, to the broad affirmation of delight as an expression of human dignity and Christian prosperity in the faith. Augustine's hard division between use and enjoyment, softened somewhat by Protestantism and later Renaissance Catholicism, now crumbled almost completely. This involved a radical and really amazing change of attitude—not just toward capitalism, but toward the whole spirit and ethos of middle-class life. Many Christians came to believe that, contrary to all traditional theology, the new middle-class life was the epitome of being Christian! The reason for this was something more profound than mere acquisitiveness, rationalization and blind conformity with the culture. We often take it for granted to the extent of forgetting that these new institutions of government, learning and business had done the unimaginable. They had liberated whole populations of human beings from tyranny and poverty. And this had happened in the most remarkable way. In the New World, capitalism made it possible for the first time to think of *gain* without doing so at the expense of others. As Walter Lippmann noted, it made it possible for the first time in history to gain in such a way that it actually served and brought benefits to society.[42]

For a time, then, both Protestants and Catholics were so critical of the middle class that historians today write of what was then viewed as the "bourgeois heresy."[43] Christian moralists launched broadsides against involvement in business, with its acquisitiveness and dependence on lines of credit and speculative investment. The whole way of life was pictured as unseemly for good Christian people. But in spite of many problems and abuses (such as the child labor system in England) that Christians roundly and rightly condemned, this stance simply could not last. As Lippmann wrote, "So it was not until the industrial revolution had altered the traditional mode of life that the vista was opened at the end of which men could see the possibility of the Good Society on this earth."[44]

Many Christians came to believe that America was not just a "new nation," it was a new *creation*, and that Americans were not just a "people" but were (to use Lincoln's phrase) "an almost *chosen* people." English writer G. K. Chesterton captured well the spirit of this theology. "Property is merely the art of democracy. It means that every man should have something that he can shape in his own image, as he is shaped in the image of Heaven."[45] The traditional Christian approval of private property had been grounded in the doctrine of human dignity and love. It now gained enormous power through this modern connection with personal liberty and as the expression of bodily life in this world as a creature (and whole nation) under God.

But what basis was there in Scripture for this original "theology of liberation"? The answer was in something that had been mostly dormant since the early Middle Ages. Christians rediscovered the literal teaching of their Old Testament. More precisely, they rediscovered its vision of human dominion on earth and this-worldly blessing. Their sense of liberation from bondage and to freedom for life in a land "flowing with milk and honey" resonated with the stories of creation and of Israel's exodus from Egypt into the Promised Land. God's dealings with Israel in Scripture seemed to illumine their own experience in the New World. By strong analogy, America was a New Israel and Americans (provided they kept the faith) would receive the first fruits of the kingdom of God—on earth.[46]

Some critics complain today that the shift was purely secular.[47] On the contrary, the Puritans and many other modern Christians remained steadfastly loyal to the Bible and to orthodox habits and beliefs. Almost all the elements of ancient Christian tradition that we have looked at remained, even though they were recast in a new light. The shift had to do more with the status of the material world in the Christian vision. The church had always affirmed the material world as God's good creation, and it had always judged possessions to be the extension of that good order. But as we have seen, Christian teaching since Augustine had also tended to draw a moral contrast between the simple enjoyment of wealth and its right use.

In New World theology the tendency was the opposite. Gone were the moral scruples about money making through credit and investment banking and through other forms of buying and selling for profit. Gone it seems was the classical "theology of the cross." In its place was a theology of guarded, morally rigorous triumph. The world was no mere theater or stage that would soon simply pass away. It was the Christian's true home and domain. Christians also pointed to other important uses, such as charity toward the poor. This went with their triumphal optimism about actually alleviating poverty one day— not just giving alms and resigning themselves to its existence. However, because of their new experience and fresh reading of Scripture, their moral instincts were not utilitarian. Their principles were more flexible and conducive to individual freedom of conscience: we must be "right" with God and with our neighbors, as Edwards put it. Those conditions being satisfied, the enjoyment of wealth was simply the enjoyment of God's gift. Such enjoyment was good.

From Augustine to the theology of the New World, Christian teaching remained constant on very basic matters. Christians through the ages have affirmed the goodness of the material world, the basic goodness of property and the inherent rights of individual persons to live lives commensurate with their dignity as human persons in the image of God. Still there has been great change and metamorphosis. The idea of true saintliness began with the monastic life "outside" the economic world as ideal. Under Protestantism the idea shifted toward life "inside" this world, except that the saint kept critical distance from the emerging world of business. In the New World the saint became almost identical with the honest, godly merchant at work in *God's* new economic order. In this culture the productive merchant exemplified the Christian "good life." So it would remain until very recent times.

The Present Debate on the Good Life: Enjoyment or Proper Use?

The present climate seems dominated by two extremes. On the one side is the popular American religion that has evolved from the New World affirmation of the culture. Christian bookstores are filled with a simple theology of triumph. This has descended in various ways from the social circumstances that we have just described. Everywhere it seems we find the presumption that the American system is God's system, and that if we work the system properly God will make us prosper. We find "biblical" manuals on "how to get rich." Popular teachers claim that if we just push the right spiritual buttons God will bless us with riches. True faith will automatically bring worldly success. It seems that we have the worldliness, the godly individualism and materialism, but without nuances. One of the more popular preachers of this "wealth gospel" is Zig Ziglar, who offers a combination of faith in Jesus with sound business practice—a formula for nearly sure success.[48] Erstwhile presidential candidate and televangelist Pat Robertson recently made a statement that illustrates perfectly the presumed relation of cause and effect between faith and wealth: "This is a good year to get right with God and become solvent."[49] The currency of this message comes from the experience of success in a rich land; it may also reflect a larger cultural loss of nuance and "literacy." Sometimes its appeal relies on sincere, undereducated and underprivileged sectors of society (often minorities) whose hunger for success makes them vulnerable to unnuanced claims in much the same way as they are to gambling on the lottery.

Meanwhile, it is rare indeed to find any mention in the preaching of how the righteous may, like Job, suffer, or the wicked prosper. It is rare to hear chronicled the inequities in our society, or of real compassion for the poor of the world, the evils we have perpetrated on them, or what our obligations to them thus might be beyond telling them, too, to become Christians and prosper. Instead, a spirit of extreme individualism and nationalism seems to prevail in much of fundamentalism and popular evangelicalism.

Justified or not, in intellectual circles one finds a fierce reaction against Western models, especially those in the popular Christian subculture. Liberation theology, with its origins in European universities (especially French) and its passion for the poor (usually in underdeveloped lands) has established winning and powerful appeal in certain segments of the church. Although its representatives address mainly the concerns of Latin America and other Third World places, it has gained popularity among Christian leaders in North America and elsewhere in the developed nations.[50] Against the theology of "health and wealth" through working the capitalist system in faith, liberation theology has revived the historic European traditions of austerity, utilitarianism and often even communalism on a social scale. The social mechanism its advocates propose is usually state control over economies and the distribution of wealth. They hope that we can liberate the poor through personal lives of solidarity with them by bringing about new political structures that guarantee economic justice. The central theme is redemption of the poor. Liberation theologians call rich Christians to remember that the prophets demand justice and that Jesus commands us to follow him by identifying with the poor.[51] The message (especially in its North American forms) has also revived the tradition of Christian hostility toward the middle class and its vision of "the good life."[52]

And so at last we come back to our original question about moral beliefs, and about our essential spirituality. Our survey of Christian tradition has helped us to put the present crisis into some perspective. It helps us to see that both the main competing Christian views are variations on different historic traditions. It also helps us to see that both are in need of careful examination and critique.[53]

It is time now to begin our exploration of Scripture and to bring our questions to its pages. Scripture will help us to construct both this critique and the fresh vision of economic life that we so badly need.

3

WE LIVE
IN A
MATERIAL
WORLD

And this most honest being, the self, speaks of the body and still wants the body, even when it . . . flutters with broken wings. It learns to speak ever more honestly, and the more it learns, the more words and honors it finds for body and earth.

FRIEDRICH NIETZSCHE, Thus Spake Zarathustra

*I*n most matters of Christian theology, we must begin our quest for answers at the beginning—with Genesis. No other beginning will do. For the other great biblical narratives all speak in the language given by Genesis. The books of the law, the prophets and wisdom, and even the gospels and epistles of the New Testament are so thoroughly immersed in the vision of Genesis that they cannot be comprehended in any depth apart from it.[1]

It might at first seem strange that an exploration into economic life should begin with Genesis. For the creation story itself is not about the use and enjoyment of wealth. Nor is it about economics or money or jobs. It does not teach us how much to spend at the mall, or whether it is right or wrong to be rich in an age of hunger. What it does, though, is offer a vision, or a way of "seeing" the world, that shapes and controls our beliefs about economic life. It gives us an *economic vision.*

The biblical story of creation offers a way of seeing the realm of nature and material things. This is part of its function as God's Word. If we are to know how to handle material things such as houses, cars and cedar decks, then we must know how to think about the more basic realm of matter itself. Is matter good? Is it evil? Is it unreal, or is it ultimate? All the world's religions and philosophies know that they must answer these questions.

The worldview of Genesis was a dramatic departure from the typical origin myths.[2] First, it made the line between God and God's creation much sharper than what was customary among the ancients. This had profound effects. It changed the external world from an awesome, divine "Thou," as ancient peoples believed it was, into a realm that was impersonal, an "It-world," more as we modern people are used to thinking of nature. Second, Genesis darkened the line between human beings and all other creatures. It gave human beings supremacy in dignity and value over everything else in creation. These two lines would eventually create a way of "seeing" the world as something to master through science, technology and other institutions of civilization, such as capitalism. Third, Genesis affirmed the material realm and bodily life in this world as "very good." This included robust affirmations of human work, cultivation, productivity and the enjoyment of life in its most physical sense of fruitfulness and abundance. Fourth, the story testifies to the fallenness and brokenness of human beings, creation and culture. With its "Yes!" to life in the world comes also a "No!" We must try to grasp each of these powerful ideas and to see them together as a coherent whole. For I believe that this constellation of truths remains fairly constant as a unified vision throughout the Old Testament. The question of whether it is upheld by Jesus and the New Testament will come later.

God's No: The Twilight of the Gods

Christian books and articles today warn us against making an idol of wealth. Indeed Christian scholarship (and scholarship in general) reminds us that American culture has become intensely selfish and materialistic.[3] All Christians ought to be troubled by this judgment. Perhaps we have forgotten just how passionately, and often, the law, the prophets, Jesus and Paul all warn about mammon. Selfish materialism is a crime against God; whole nations have fallen, says Scripture, because of it. But just what is selfish materialism? How do we know it when we see it? As we have already seen, Christians speak with one voice in condemning injustice and greed, but we are divided on the crucial matter of what makes certain actions unjust and/or covetous. Is or is not our proverbial person on the backyard deck in urban America guilty of greed and injustice for delighting in abundance? Genesis can provide the sharpening of eye that we badly need for answering such questions.

Most scholars agree that the ancient Hebrews were the first people to develop a religion of true "transcendence." In other words, they were the first to picture God as altogether "above" and "beyond" nature. Their God was not to be confused at all with the creation. Images of God were fiercely forbidden. Thus, as mentioned above, they were the first people whose religion demoted the material world from its status as a divine "Thou" to the status of a nondivine "It."[4]

In contrast, the myths of the great ancient nations show that they adored the sun, moon and stars, and they believed that all of what we call nature was a world of living, personal, divine self-consciousness, a realm of movement, will and activity. In our terms, nature was a personal agent, a "Thou," comprising many "thous." That is one reason why people of the myths often showed much greater reverence for the nonhuman world than we are accustomed to showing in our culture. For example, Native Americans believed that the land, plants and animals were personal beings, with their own inherent rights to exist and to flourish, and to be treated with respect. Many moderns have come to see that there is great beauty and ancient power in this way of seeing. We sense that it possesses something that we have lost in our detached Western-European way of looking at nature. In each of us, if we are attuned to it, is a song of lament for the lost soul of the earth spirits, the Buffalo People, and the great Thunder Beings who gave visions to the ones who looked and listened for them in the lightning and rain with their whole inner being. I dare say that no modern housewife, banker, insurance salesperson, doctor, lawyer, graduate student, minister or even tenured college professor is so thoroughly dulled by civilization that he or she cannot feel its native power to arouse nostalgia for a lost, primitive and in some ways better, time.

Nevertheless, like it or not, such reverence for nature came at a heavy price. For the mythic peoples, this way of seeing gave them no clear way of telling the difference in status or value between humans, animals, nature and the gods.[5] This made it very difficult to sustain distinctions that we now take for granted as the groundings of civilized existence—the majesty of God, the dignity and value of individual humans, the subordination of animals and nature to humans, among other things.

It was not always so with us. We owe our basic groundviews to the Hebrews. Scholars agree that Genesis purposely aimed its polemics at the myths and attempted to carve clear lines from the blurred vision of ancient humankind. A prime example of this "carving" is in its remarkable treatment of light. The ancients had always worshiped light, especially as connected with the sun, the moon and the stars. Light was the life energy of all things. Existence was impossible without it. In all the religions the absence of light—darkness—was practically synonymous with demonic evil. However, without due warning, Genesis stepped onto the stage of human history with new words for a new language on the earth: "Then God said, 'Let there be light'; and there was light." We need to hear these words anew, with the open-mouthed astonishment of an ancient man or woman. The God of Genesis commands that there be light, and the "god" of light obeys—absolutely. There *was* light. Before the all-powerful God of Genesis, light cannot be called a god. It has been dedivinized (although perhaps not desacralized, as we shall see). God can in no way be confused with light, or light with God. A few verses later the author reports almost as an afterthought that God "made the two great lights . . . and the stars" (Gen 1:16). Sun, moon and stars go to their subordinate places in the nonpersoned "It-world." They go to serve God, human beings and the earth, not to rule them. This was, in Nietzsche's words, "the twilight of the gods."

Our first theme, then, is the rise of the new God who declares the material world, from top to bottom, to be a nonpersoned, nondivine "It." Even though we shall speak later of the sacredness and preciousness of nature in biblical terms, it is true to a great extent that the Bible takes the living soul from the world. The theme of God's "otherness," or transcendence, thus brings with it a commanding "No!" to idolatry, to use Karl Barth's famous term.

God's transcendent "No!" has immense importance to our search for economic identity. One side of this is obvious and has received much attention lately. In its broad terms, the warning is indisputable and real. As Jesus bluntly put it, standing in a long line of biblical prophets, "You cannot serve God and wealth."

But the warning provokes a question that must not be answered too soon. Let us not decide too quickly what it is that *makes* the enjoyment of wealth godless, or idolatrous. Most answers end up being too simplistic. They often seize upon the "No!" without also hearing the "Yes!" to the creation that it both conceals and reveals.

God's Yes to the World: Royal Man and Woman on the Sacred Earth
We mentioned earlier that the "No!" in Genesis also contains a "Yes!"

Our fear, worship and ultimate devotion must be given to the transcendent King of the universe. In that way Genesis indeed closes nature off to religious worship. Because nature is no longer our lord and master, it loses its living soul. Yet this negation of nature worship makes room for a kind of affirmation that seemed impossible within the world of myth: nature becomes an *object,* and thus something to be approached without religious awe or fear. It may thus be explored, studied, cultivated, tamed, exploited, used and enjoyed.

Both defenders and critics of Christianity agree that this demystification of nature helped to give the "green light" to the aggressive movement in science, technology and economic life that we associate with Western civilization.[6] It is true that the Western mentality is to some extent rooted in the biblical way of seeing the world. The mentality of mastery over nature is strengthened by the biblical teaching that God made humankind in his very image and likeness, that God gave human beings dominion over the earth and its inhabitants, commanded them to "be fruitful and multiply, and fill the earth and subdue it" (Gen 1:28). The very assertion of these claims today (understandably) invites wrath from ecologically passionate people.[7] Seldom before has it been so urgent that Christians understand and articulate their own theology of human dominion in the context of nature and economic life. It will do no good, and great harm, simply to avoid asserting human dominion, but what kind of dominion is envisioned?

Ancient peoples searched desperately for a clear sense of identity. Like us, they asked the basic questions, "Who are we?" "What is man?" "Why are we here?" "What is life all about?" Their answer was often pretty grim. The Babylonian creation story, *Enuma Elish,* taught that human beings were made to bear the burdens of the gods.[8] Life had taught them that being human, at least for the vast majority, was hard. If there was real hope it was in an afterlife—and even that became doubtful for some. Many people today can identify with the world-weariness of the ancients.

But Genesis offers a contrast to the ancient pattern and to our modern burnout with life. It certainly agrees that life is a hard business. A person shall live and eat bread only "by the sweat of [one's] face." But thorns, thistles and all those things that make us sweat (and sometimes bleed) for every inch of dignity are not the most basic metaphors of human existence for Genesis. The very first picture of human identity is rather that God made us in his own image! "Then God said, 'Let us make humankind in our image, according to our likeness' " (Gen 1:26).

Just what this language means has been the subject of many theories and debates.[9] But let us return for a moment to the ancient horizon of the text for some help in getting at the core of its meaning. We have seen that the mythic peoples had no clear lines between God, humans and nature. This meant that their sense of the religious and moral order contained nothing like our idea of human supremacy, dignity and value. As we have seen, the distinctions between gods, humans, plants, animals and so forth were flexible and blurred by our common standards. This lack of clear lines, especially about where humankind fit into the spectrum of things, was reflected in the social and political structures. Ancient societies all understood themselves to be agents of divine power.[10] The greater the power, the greater (and more important) were the people. The center of that power, which validated the people, was the earthly monarch. The gods executed their will on earth through the king or queen. The ruling monarch was thus the incarnate presence of god—he or she embodied the power of the sun, the moon and the stars. The blurred lines allowed divinity, and in this sense celestial power, to the king or queen. The status of the rest of humankind was not on that plane, nor was it clearly demarcated from or elevated above that of other beings.

Therefore, it is crucial for the biblical reader to know that the Egyptians referred to their pharaoh as "the image of God." The Assyrians, too, referred to their king as being "god's very image."[11] It seems that the author(s) of Genesis purposely used a known idiom to express and reveal an idea that was yet unknown in their time.

> Then God said, "Let us make humankind in our image, according to our likeness; and let them have dominion over the fish of the sea, and over the birds of the air, and over the cattle, and over all the wild animals of the earth, and over every creeping thing that creeps upon the earth." (Gen 1:26)

As von Rad put it, "Just as powerful earthly kings, to indicate their claim and dominion, erect an image of themselves in the provinces of their empire, . . . so man is placed upon earth in God's image as God's sovereign emblem."[12] By stating that God made humans in his image, the author gave all human beings a royal identity comparable to that of a pharaoh, king or queen, as well as royal obligations commensurate with the role. That is to say, all human beings have this authoritative status before God, and are thus called on to represent on earth God's rule over heaven. To be made in God's image most basically means to have been given dominion over the earth, under God. Much is promised here—not just the supremacy of humankind, but the rudiments of what would become our modern ideas concerning the dignity and "inalienable rights" of *every* human person. (In fact it is difficult to downplay the idea of human supremacy without also weakening the ideology of human rights.)

In Genesis, then, human identity is expressed first in the language of royal dominion and calling. Unlike ancient myth, this language does not deify human beings—we are not to act as gods—but it does dignify and bless the whole race with the highest creaturely status possible. The language of representation also requires conformity with the will of the One who created them and placed them on earth. Their realm of rule is ultimately not their kingdom, but God's. Their dominion derives from God's.

The peculiar theme of dominion is thus the dominant one in this part of the story. God blesses the first humans and then commands them to go forth to "fill the earth and subdue it" (Gen 1:28).[13] The image is one of a God-derived freedom, dignity, power and royal effect over the whole earth and its inhabitants. There is a fundamental repudiation of any religion or theory that puts human beings on the same plane as God, but also, on the other hand, on a level equal with or below the various elements of nature—earth, animals, plants, sun, moon or stars. Human beings are not gods, but they are lords, the lords of God over nature.

It is well known, if taken for granted, that our whole tradition of human rights and equality stems from the belief that human beings uniquely bear God's image and likeness. All of the great modern liberation movements have born great passion for the royal man and woman. The language of liberty is in essence the language of dominion in its positive form, a language that we, then, dare not forget.

But the language of Genesis is so strong that, as we have mentioned, some critics blame it for our ecological and social problems.[14] If there are compelling reasons to affirm human supremacy, there is also much against doing so. The global ecological crisis is explained in part as a failure of our Western view with its anthropocentric, detached and brutal lack of reverence for nature. We will hardly destroy a redwood forest if we believe that the great trees are a people with a divine nature and purpose. Native Americans could not imagine wiping out the buffalo by strangling its range with barbed wire and shooting the remnant for its hides—or just for sporting fun. We can accuse the primitive cultures of many evils, but not of this wanton savagery against nature. That seems destined to be our pathetic legacy as Western European "Christians." If not our biblical view of nature, what made us capable of doing these things? Does the passion for the royal man and woman necessarily cause the destruction of nature in pursuit of our economic life?

Genesis 1 describes pictorially the quality of power that human beings are to represent on earth. The six days of creation give us a picture of God using his great power. In its mammoth quantity, as we have seen, the effects of this power are staggering. This is power in its maximal form, beyond anything we can well imagine. But it is also "positive power." In its quality, it is the quintessence of the very opposite of the demonic. The God of Genesis first creates out of sheer delight in the goodness of his creation. The classical doctrine that says that God created to "glorify himself" is very misleading and has led to many unfortunate sermons and catechism lessons about "God everything, human beings nothing." Of course it is to God's glory that he creates, but when he creates he both enriches himself *and* glorifies everyone and everything else. By his power God frees, orders and empowers other beings to be themselves, to be what is closest to their essences as individual beings, as parts of a cosmic whole. In his royal greatness, God uses power to liberate other beings from "nothingness" to an existence that is "good." Unlike the power we may see around us, God's power expresses itself in sovereign, royal love.

If some communities today fail to appreciate God's power, others have often not appreciated the servant form that is its glory.[15] The delight of God is "other-centered," rather than "self-centered." His joy is comparable to that of an artist in the sheer rightness and integrity of an artwork, or of a parent in the birth of a strong and vigorously healthy child. His joy is in a world completely in harmony with itself, everything in its proper place, shalom. For the sun, moon and stars, God made the heavens and light. For the fish and birds, he designed the seas and the sky. For plants, animals and humans, God made the dry land. Everything was in its place, and that place was *good* for every being described. And the whole creation was "very good." In this sense, the God of power in Genesis 1 is also a servant of his creatures. He rules. But he also serves with great passion and compassion. His rule empowers and magnifies his subjects. It does not oppress or diminish them. Such is the model of dominion that is presupposed in the language of Genesis about human rule and dominion over the earth. God's lordly passion for his world makes us royal and supreme, but in such a way that it also makes our earth sacred. God's "Yes!" to human beings as rulers includes within it a "Yes!" to the whole cosmos and everything in it created by God. In the simple language of the text, it is "very good."

Whatever human dominion is in Genesis, then, it ennobles us for the purpose of ennobling everyone and everything else. We, too, are servants in royal form. Human beings were not made primarily to rule over each other, but to be coworkers, in mutual respect, representing God's kingdom on earth.[16] This predemocratic idea follows from reverence for the royal dignity of every individual.[17] Moreover, God made human beings from the earth, in solidarity with the earth, and he placed them in the Garden "to till it and keep it" (Gen 2:15). As the later history of Israel and the land will show, Genesis and Native American thought have much more in common on the sacredness of the land and its inhabitants than either tradition has typically acknowledged. Pollution of the land and the wanton destruction of animal and plant life ought to be just as great a sacrilege and desecration to Christians as it is to Native American people, although for somewhat disparate reasons. While insisting on the supremacy of human beings, the dominion theology of Christians must at once also be a rich source of energy for a fierce environmentalism.

In sum, our use of power must be in character and quality like God's use of power. As God empowers us, we empower everyone and everything else, according to the order of creation. In relation to God, it dignifies without deifying us; in relation to each other, it empowers us to empower others as our coequals in dignity and worth; in relation to nature, it gives us supremacy over a realm that is itself sacred.

Godly Materialism, Dominion and Delight
As suggested earlier, human dominion in Genesis also expresses itself in the language of productive work, abundance, flourishing and de-

light. There is a sorrowfulness about ancient civilization. Much of this sorrow came from the profound awareness that we humans are finite in our mortal flesh. Something in our human longing for eternity, expressed in our greatest cultural achievements, finds our existence in time and space, inside these mortal bodies of ours, troublesome and prisonlike. We feel like birds with our wings clipped. Perhaps this is the reason why religions so often tend toward otherworldliness and spiritualism.

To an extent, this ancient problem is at the root of our current search for economic integrity. Both Thomas Jefferson and Karl Marx rejected a fully biblical Christianity because they believed it was too otherworldly. They echoed the sentiments of Nietzsche when he declared that, in essence, Christians were "haters of the body" and "the great despisers of the earth." They are incapable of unqualified delight in the fruits of the earth, like the devout portrayed so vividly in the modern film *Babette's Feast*.

Such Christians did not hear very well what Karl Barth called God's "Yes!" to the creation. Throughout Genesis 1 the text affirms the material world as both real and "good" (an affirmation that is repeated throughout the story)—as something that truly ought to be. To the world of light, land, sky and seas, the heavenly cosmos and the earthly collection of plants and animals, God gives a joyous blessing. Like an artist, he gazes admiringly on the whole creation and is pleased to say that it—all of it—is "very good" (Gen 1:31). I suggest that the goodness of the world is not just the ground concept for rules about respecting the earth; it is also about its capacities to bring royal delight to human beings. It is about the cosmic harmony that is received in delight by human beings. The goodness of the creation that Genesis 1 describes is simply unthinkable apart from its abundant and varied spectrum of material properties. These are as essential to the goodness of the created order as the physical body is to a *fully* human identity.[18] The common idiom that says that we *have* bodies is not quite consistent with the imagery of Genesis 2. It is more appropriate to say that, as fully and operationally human beings, we are bodily beings, created for material life.[19]

This point is illustrated in Genesis 2:7-9, where God forms the man from the ground and places him like a small king in a pleasure garden with all its delights. The idea is "earthy" and wonderfully extravagant. Human beings are "earth beings"—of, by and for the earth. We are fashioned from the earth to live upon the earth, to dominate, cultivate and care for the earth—*and* to use and *enjoy* the fruits of the earth. *All* of this is included in the sense of dominion that springs from the narrative. The whole person, who works, conserves, cultivates, nourishes, protects, but also does so as the one who rules, orders, dominates and simply enjoys at his or her good pleasure, is the original, majestic human being. Such a person is indeed a "steward" of creation and a "servant," but such terms are inadequate quite to identify the royal man or royal woman of Genesis's vision. It is as if we were to describe the biblical David as "a man whom God appointed to care for his people." The statement would be true, but it would not identify David as the great, royal person that he was—the king of Israel.

It is true that we are more than mere bodies, and that we are also spiritual beings. God breathes his breath into the first human and brings him to spiritual life. We are rational, moral beings, and much else besides. But our fullest spiritual, rational and moral capacities are not easily imagined apart from the body and bodily action, and ultimately apart from *majesty* of a physical sort. The experience of physical majesty is the experience of human freedom in the real world. That is why, for the ancient Hebrew, life apart from the body was not "life" at all, but mere existence. The quintessential vision of life in its full expression is the physical person in the garden of delight.

Genesis 2 teaches us that bodily life is essentially good. The story pictures this goodness in the setting of an oriental pleasure garden, lush with fruit and vegetation, teeming with life of all sorts, its beauties enriched by the flowing of the four great rivers from its heart. The man and the woman lived with royal effect, and that was good. These are images of creative, productive and fruitful work (and the obligations that go with being human). But with that, they are pictures of enjoyment and pure delight in the world. They are pictures of blessing for self-actualizing freedom to enjoy life as a gift. We shall talk of limits later, for the serpent forces us to concentrate on the "limits" that God has placed on us. But the divine permission, "You are free to eat from any tree of the garden," expresses more than concern for mere nourishment or adequate nutrition, so that, "scraping by," we can be good workers and stewards and inherit the many duties and obligations that come with these roles. Rather, it conveys the vast, superfluous horizon of freedom for delight that God gave to human beings in the beginning. The whole view is one of almost embarrassingly extravagant delight and excess. God gave them not just the conditions for functional existence, but the conditions for majesty—within limits of course. Genesis presents a challenge to the time-honored (and somewhat popular) Christian tendency to equate enjoyment of the superfluous with greediness and injustice. There is an enjoyment in the superfluous that is very good.

This helps us to picture the kind of bodily life that is good. Not just any such life is good in the strong sense of the creation story. The picture of life in the Garden is not just an attack on poverty, although it is implicitly that. It is also an assault on meagerness. The expression "fit for a king" is appropriate here. The entire material existence of the man and the woman is one of unashamed splendor. That they were naked and not ashamed confirms the pure, direct and unspoiled relationship that they had with the world of physical delight. The story impresses on us that abundance, fruitfulness, excess and delight are the proper conditions for a full life. And it forces us to make a distinction that is too seldom made—between the carnal lust of hedonism and the dignity of royal delight that God blesses. In our fallen world is a false delight that is dark, demonic and evil. And the prophets will later help us to identify this kind of gratification for what it is. But true delight is "very good." Indeed, it summarizes the right relationship between human beings and the world. Far from being opposed to compassion and servanthood, as is commonly supposed, delight is compassion's child. The suggestion here is that true delight is what good people ought to wish for all people of the earth, including themselves. Delight, rather than mere sustenance, ought to be our guiding vision while seeking liberation for the poor.[20]

Because of the enormous resistance to this point in some circles (and also the oversimplified and unnuanced acceptance of it in others), we must explore it a little further. There is something wrong and doubly tragic about a poor and broken king. That is what makes so many fairy tales so very powerful. It is also behind the sorrow and grief that flow from almost every story in the Gospel accounts of Jesus. He is the true Royal Man who has been separated from his proper majesty and royal effect. This creates a sense of injustice and frustration—even outrage—in the reader. When the true king is at last raised up and reunited with his kingdom and proper royal effects—glory, laud and honor, a seat at the head of the table of great feasts—we feel that the right nature of things has been restored, the moral order of the universe has been satisfied, and joy returns. We can go in the peace of true shalom.

This means that the "luxuries" and "superfluousness" that utilitarian ethics condemn may actually be strange "necessities" in the world of Genesis. Shakespeare's great genius makes this connection in *King Lear*. The old king unwisely gives his kingdom away to his daughters before he dies, but he continues trying to maintain his royal dignity. So he employs a large court of servants and bodyguards at some cost. His soul-barren daughter chastens him for the superfluous expenses. Being "every inch a king," Lear fiercely resists her utilitarian logic:

O, reason not the need: our basest beggars are in the poorest things superfluous: Allow not nature more than nature needs, man's life is cheap as beast's.[21]

Lear knows that he is waging war for the human soul. There is a difference between his love of royal effect or majesty and his daughter's lust for money and things. As the great psychologist William James wrote:

> Man's chief difference from the brutes lies in the exuberant excess of his subjective propensities. His preeminence over them lies simply and solely in the fantastic and unnecessary character of his wants, physical, moral, aesthetic and intellectual. Had his whole life not been a quest for the superfluous, he would never have established himself so inexpungeably in the necessary. . . . Prune down his extravagances, sober him, and you undo him.[22]

To the extent that Christian tradition and recent Christian moral theology has been negative toward individualism expressed in enjoyment of the superfluous, I believe we must think again.

I was driving through an American suburban neighborhood the other day. It was a bright, sunlit early evening. Some people were working in their yards, raking, mowing, repairing things, painting, scraping, gardening. Others were just sitting back, surveying their premises, absorbing the moment—like kings and queens. It is too true (and too easy to see) that there are deficiencies in suburban America. What struck me that evening, though, and caused me quite unexpectedly to be deeply moved, was the fierce, regal desire for human dignity that came through it all. If we look sympathetically, do we not behold something of the awakened kings and queens in the human spirit? Beneath the questionable values that dictate choosing the best jobs and locating ourselves in the "good" neighborhoods, behind the huge investments in home environment, beyond the incessant mowing, pruning and beautifying, do we not see the great spirit awakened two centuries ago by the American Revolution? The first "liberation theology" was our Founding Fathers' prophetic voice against European monarchy and tyranny. They proclaimed democratic, individual freedom to pursue life, liberty and (material) happiness. It is not coincidental that Thomas Jefferson built his model on one of the few sections of the Bible that he still admired—the story of creation.[23]

The creation story suggests that physical and material delightfulness (superfluity) is needed for healthy human self-esteem. It is no doubt why delightful physical actions like getting in good shape, buying a fine new dress or suit, having one's hair done well or getting behind the wheel of a finely tuned car elevate us from various states of depression and discouragement. The same is true of sitting in front of a fire on a cold winter evening and grilling steaks on cedar decks on a warm spring evening. Perhaps that is why Jesus praised and immortalized the woman who (to the horror of Judas Iscariot) poured a whole jar of pure nard, costing a year's income, over his head to waft beautifully through the room for only a few moments of intense beauty and delight in his presence (Jn 12:3).

Although the issue is complicated, and we will have much more to say about it in later chapters, the story of Genesis makes clear that not all excess and extravagance is wantonness. Not all "who come eating and drinking," as Jesus did, are "drunkards and gluttons." Human delight is a precious expression of God's glory, human dignity and the goodness of life in this world. In its proper form it is a sacrament to God's dominion over chaos and darkness.

The Power of the Serpent

The words "You are free to eat from any tree in the garden" are about God's blessing and our freedom. The Creator gave human beings the run of the place. Nevertheless, with freedom comes limit and responsibility. There is deadly danger in the Garden of delight: "But of the tree of the knowledge of good and evil you shall not eat, for in the day that you eat of it you shall die" (Gen 2:17). The serpent, twisting the truth, hisses: "You will not die; for God knows that when you eat of it your eyes will be opened, and you will be like God, knowing good and evil" (Gen 3:4-5). At this point the woman discovers an altogether new form of pleasure. It is pleasure in a new fruit, the fruit of the "knowledge of good and evil." The power of attraction is too great and she and her husband both eat. God's judgment over this disaster confirms the serpent's horrible half-truth: "The man has become like one of us, knowing good and evil" (Gen 3:22).

According to Malcolm Clark, the idiom of knowing good and evil was "judicial," that is, about rightful authority to make judgments.[24] His careful research confirms the traditional view of the Fall as a quest for equality with God. The man and woman wished to be their own gods, little miniature "Yahwehs," autonomous rulers of their own universe.

This story is no mere history lesson. It is a warning to the whole human race. "Sin" means that we have pulled ourselves away from God and made ourselves into "gods," knowing good and evil for ourselves. After eating from the tree of knowledge, the man and the woman run away to hide from God. That is the essence of negative power. It isolates the self from all things that are good in life. It is death. We pull ourselves apart from each other. The man blames the woman for his troubles and becomes a petty dictator in the marriage. The woman suffers pain in childbearing and must endure great vulnerability to abuse at home. We pull ourselves apart from our true home, the earth, which is "cursed" because of what we have done (Gen 3:17). Thorns and thistles emerge from cracked soil. Drops of sweat break from the brow. Work thus becomes hard and tiresome. After Cain murders Abel and God banishes him from the land, cities emerge as a poor substitute. The essence of Enoch, Babel, Sodom and Gomorrah is our alienation from nature. These seem at first false worlds, antiworlds, miscreations (although God redeems them).

In sum, the majesty and royal effect of human dominion seems lost. The man had been created *from* the ground, in solidarity with the ground, to have dominion over the ground. Now at his inaugural moment of triumph, he is lost in the dust of death: "you are dust, and to dust you shall return." In physical death, the ground arises in dominion over the man. The reversal is complete. The earth is a kingdom on the run toward ruin.

But here the story takes an unexpected and very subtle turn. Many Christians have missed it. Some have concluded that the world, according to the Bible, has become evil, and that human beings have entirely lost their goodness.[25] Others have concluded that the evil in the world vastly outweighs the good most of the time. If that is our interpretation, then our approach to economic life in the world will show it in one way or another. Sometimes the separatism is quite literal, as with the Amish or certain communal sects. But often it is more subtle and psychological in nature. We sometimes see mainly the evil in our culture, and not the good, even when it occurs. We may not literally separate ourselves, but our basic instinct will nevertheless be countercultural, to see first of all the evils in our economic world. This may cause us to miss what is good.[26] Genesis, however, is not a separatistic or countercultural document. The author(s) fought passionately for the goodness of creation and of our humanity. The story calls us to have faith that God's creation (not just God) is stronger than any evil power that comes against it. The same is true, on the whole, with human culture, for it remains open to the good. What follows is an extraordinary effort to combine realism with hope.

Small glimpses of light flicker in the darkness. The land may be cursed, but it has not become barren—we shall still eat bread. The same is true of the woman. Her glorious role in bringing new humans into being has become painful and dangerous, but she shall still bring forth children. The marriage is in trouble and in danger of becoming a male dictatorship over a restive female clientele. But the two still cleave to one another and go on in wedlock. The only entity in the story that God treats as an evil in itself is the serpent. The Chaos

Bringer, the Destroyer of Worlds, will inflict damage, but the son of the woman will crush his head. The tone is one of hard and distant victory in a mood of persistent hope. Considering the otherworldliness and resignation of some religions, there is remarkably strong passion for life in the narrative. It simply refuses to surrender to the darkness.

The story continues to reveal evil doing its worst to destroy the integrity of humankind, the earth and everything in it. Nevertheless, the righteousness of Noah stands. Like a boulder in a stream, nothing can move him. Because of him the floods of chaos purify rather than destroy the world. Through him the cosmic order, including all the animals, is restored rather than wiped out by chaos. And through him the moral order of creation is restored rather than entirely corrupted by sin. The world order and the moral order (including the moral integrity and value of human beings) are redeemed and reestablished forever. Noah's role is defined at birth. His father says, "Out of the ground that the LORD has cursed this one shall bring us relief from our work and from the toil of our hands" (Gen 5:29). From here the narrative moves lightly, gently and upward against the oppressive weight of the Fall, until it reaches the dry land of a new beginning.

Hope in the Real World

Genesis 9 is one of the most important (though neglected) chapters in the Bible. The covenant with Noah reestablishes the essential order of creation. It also recognizes the stubborn presence of disorder and sin. Unlike the world of Genesis 1, the world of Genesis 9 is a system of both good and evil. The good is primary, but the evil is most seriously real.

If Genesis 1 shows us the world as it ought to be, Genesis 9 comes closer to showing the world as it really is. The real world is not just God's good creation—it is God's good but *fallen* creation. This view of the world makes programs of simple world-denial or world-affirmation seem shallow. Either they ignore the "Yes!" that remains of our createdness, or they ignore the "No!" of our brokenness.

The end of Noah's story and the covenant that God makes with him bring out this very complex picture of a good world tainted by evil. We must try to picture this ourselves, because a morally sound economic life must be faithful to God's ideal will for us, and it must be fiercely honest, truthful and realistic about human good and evil. By extension, a morally sound economic theory or system would be one that best conserved and promoted the right ideals with truthfulness and integrity—in the real world.

Genesis 9 helps us to see how good and evil now coexist in a kind of order. God sends Noah from the ark with "every living thing" to return to the dry land. There the creation blessing is given once again: "Be fruitful and multiply, and fill the earth" (Gen 9:1). God promises, "I will never again curse the ground because of humankind" (Gen 8:21). The ground is again established as God's good, precious, sacred creation, and so it will remain to the end. Then God reinstitutes the dominion of human beings over the earth, although there is a new twist. Dominion over the animals is now marked by "dread" on their part. The new order is also marked by the rightful killing and eating of animals in addition to the plants. "Every moving thing that lives shall be food for you" (Gen 9:3). Moreover, God reaffirms human beings as the bearers of his own image. The undertone of ambivalence is clear. This restoration of human dignity is expressed as a necessary argument for punishing murderers. That is, ideal values are expressed grimly, without a trace of naivete, in the real, fallen world.

> Whoever sheds the blood of a human,
>> by a human shall that person's blood be shed;
> for in his own image
>> God made humankind. (Gen 9:6)

The same ambivalence comes through when Noah, like Adam, goes to his new vineyard and its delights. His enjoyment of superabundance (surely enhanced by having spent over a month on the ark) crossed over into a drunken stupor. This leads to the strange story of violation by his own son and the return of the theme of nakedness and shame. The cloying power of sin is real. The whole reaffirmation of the world admits this: "for the inclination of the human heart is evil from youth" (Gen 8:21). The world is still good, human beings are still human, the earth still brings forth, the possibility of dominion and delight is still a reality. But sin remains at the heart of our race. Still, God establishes the remarkable covenant with the entire human race, with every living creature, and with the earth itself. The covenant is universal and cosmic in scope; it expresses God's endless passion for this world even as it admits the presence of evil in the heart. The covenant is to last forever, its sign the rainbow in heaven.

The good order of God's creative word has been touched by the serpent's tongue. Genesis warns us to remember who we are, that we are dust, that we are more vulnerable than we wish to believe to a lust for negative power. It reminds us bitterly that the world lacks shalom in the truest sense and that our exercise of freedom and delight does not easily embrace love or justice. It reminds us that the quest for these virtues is difficult, elusive and (in a cosmic sense) beyond our power to fulfill. But it also reminds us that the created order has not been destroyed, that we are not alone in our efforts to restore servant dominion to the planet and to our own personal lives, and that we must keep striving for what is good and not give up on the goodness of this life.

Can there remain a godly materialism in such a world? The story of the exodus will help us on our way toward seeing how the magnificent vision of Genesis—for human beings, animals and all the earth—might be worked out in a fallen economic world.

4

LIBERTY, LUXURY
& LIBERATION
IN THE
EXODUS

Land is a central, if not the central theme, of biblical faith.
WALTER BRUEGGEMANN, The Land

Most of us learned the story of the exodus in Sunday school. And scenes from the film *The Ten Commandments* (Charlton Heston's Moses getting whiter and more god-struck with each miracle) are forever printed on our imaginations. But we may not have learned that the biblical exodus is serious theology. To ancient Hebrews the exodus was (after the creation of the world) the most important event of all time. It was the event in which the God of the universe came forth from the darkness to reveal himself to the world through Israel, his "light unto the nations." The exodus confirmed and sealed God's ancient promises to Abraham, Isaac and Jacob that he would make them into a great nation.[1] And it revealed to the world that the God of Israel was indeed the Lord of all the earth.

Today the exodus is also a very serious narrative on economic life for nations and individual persons. Many will be surprised to learn that this old Bible story inspires political and economic revolution around the planet. At the forefront, liberation theologians stress that the exodus is a world-shaking narrative about political and economic liberation. It is about the God who liberates the poor.[2] As North American writer Ron Sider reminds a Christian public that has tended to spiritualize the faith, the story of the exodus shows that "the God of the Bible wants to be known as the liberator of the oppressed."[3] The reminder is most timely, and true.

The story of the exodus indeed carries forth a basic theme of Genesis. To God, the physical world counts, and so does the physical state of human beings. Otherwise, physical misfortune and cruelty could not be the outrage in Scripture that they are. If the material conditions of life were not real or essential to the moral order, such things would merely count as unpleasant or distasteful occurrences to be endured, or perhaps ignored. But we would have no right to see them as genuine *evils* and to become morally indignant about them. Liberation theologians have made us think again about the sacredness of life in *this* world. Refusing to ignore the poverty in their cultures, they have bravely led the way of Christians to knowledge of a God who burns with righteous anger against the poverty of his children (especially when it is caused by deliberate oppression).

Third World intellectuals are also keenly sensitive to another level of the story. The exodus teaches that evil is expressed through social institutions and systems. Pietistic biblical Christians (often benefiting from social structures that are favorable to them) have too often ignored this "structural evil." The exodus is largely a tale of God's engagement with principalities and powers that have lodged themselves in oppressive political and economic systems. When this happens, the message is, God's people must seek not only "righteousness" in their private lives, but also "justice" in the social realm. Social justice is simply the cultural expression of true piety, righteousness before the Lord.[4] God's judgment fell on an oppressive economic system, and he liberated the oppressed. God then tested and molded these people into a nation, with a new *system* of religious, political and economic laws—a system anchored by an uncompromising commitment to social justice. Just as God destroyed evil institutions, we see that God involves himself in the creation of new, good ones. And he thus uses them to create and sustain liberty and justice for human beings. God liberates through the shaping of just societies. God's people must represent him in this work.

There is little debate in Christian theology today on the broader points made so far about the social meaning of the exodus. However, there is great debate on the question of just *how* God desires that we shape our societies and our personal lives.[5] The God of Scripture is the God who liberates the poor. But how? To what end and purpose? What does the liberated society or person look like? Through which habits and institutions of society do human beings experience real justice and liberty? Is there an "exodus vision" that can shape our modern lives for true goodness and justice? And how does it lead wealthy Christians to reflect on our own identities?

Exodus Vision: Life, Liberty and Property in Israel

Scholars agree that the many laws of Israel express an "exodus vision" of society. The laws are repeatedly grounded in words that Israel recited in worship: "For I am the LORD your God, who brought you out of Egypt."[6] The implication is clear. Israel's national life must reflect the character of the God who redeemed them from bondage. The God who liberates has molded a people of liberation.

Once again, the story of the exodus carries over a great theme from the story of creation and places it in the context of real economic life. God uses his great power to liberate other beings by creating them, and he makes them flourish as the beings that they truly are. Human beings were created for the purpose of representing God's servant-dominion, or kingdom, on earth. Just so, as redeemed (liberated) people, they must also be redeemers (liberators) of the poor and powerless.

The laws (many of them baffling, harsh and even senseless to the modern person) always come back to that gentle, constant refrain of God's compassion for powerless people. The law repeatedly makes special provision for the widow, the orphan, the poor, the alien and the one who sojourns without a home. Through this spirit of compassion, the vast volume of laws, too numerous and confusing to name, breathes the spirit of *God's* one true law, which requires that we love our "neighbor" as ourselves (Lev 19:18).

One of the most important and compelling sections of Scripture for understanding the exodus vision of economic life is the Holiness Code of Leviticus 17—26.[7] An especially remarkable aspect of the code is the association between holiness and the marketplace. There is indeed guidance on ceremony and devotional worship, on personal moral habits and much else besides. But its religious concerns extend with special force to Israel's *economic* life.

Many laws created a liberating force in the lives of the poor and powerless in Israel. For instance, fields were not supposed to be harvested to the margins. Landowners were to leave grain and fruit around the edges so that "the poor and the alien" might glean from the remains (Lev 19:9-10; 23:22). The Israelites were not to abuse the "stranger" or "alien," and it is in this economic context that they were commanded to "love the alien as yourself" (Lev 19:33-34). In doing business, "honest weights" and measures were to be used (Lev 19:35-37). Elsewhere, laws protected the poor from unfair lending practices. No collateral was to be required of a poor borrower, and wealthy persons were not to take advantage of needy brothers (Israelites) by charging interest on loans (Ex 22:25-27).[8]

Leviticus 25 proclaims a "sabbath" for the land on every seventh year. The purpose is not just to give the land rest, although this is sound ecology. It also aims at enhancing economic humaneness in Israel for both animals and working people. It is to provide food for "you, your male and female slaves, your hired and your bound laborers who live with you; for your livestock also, and for the wild animals in your land." Whatever the land produces is to be eaten (Lev 25:1-7). This concern for the poor and powerless (including the earth and animals) is indeed in the very soul of the law. It is essential to the whole biblical vision of delight and shalom.

Deuteronomy 15 proclaims a "year of release" every seventh year.[9] On the seventh year all loans to Israelites were simply to be canceled (Deut 15:1-6)! Furthermore, lenders were not to refuse loans to the poor just because the seventh year was soon approaching. The logic in both laws is similar: "there will . . . be no one in need among you" (Deut 15:4). But (note the realism) since "there will never cease to be some in need on the earth," they should "open [their] hand to the poor and needy neighbor in [their] land" (Deut 15:11). Hebrew slaves were also to be liberated every seventh year (Deut 15:12). Again the logic is grounded in God's actions and character. For "you were a slave in the land of Egypt, and the Lord your God redeemed you; for this reason I lay this command upon you today" (Deut 15:15).

These texts confirm that God wished his nation to be a decent society. The legal and moral system breathed a spirit of mercy, giving the poor special upward movement. Israel was never, never to forget the poor. As the prophets must later remind them, in doing so they would forget who they were, that they too were slaves, and they would thus (despite their pious rhetoric) forget God who redeemed them from bondage.

In our modern supereconomies we cannot realistically consider a slavish imitation of practices such as canceling debts every seven years. No one seriously considers this an option, because it would obviously destroy our system and its ability to empower people through the creation of jobs and so forth. The poor would suffer most from such economic devastation. Scripture calls us rather to contemplate its deeper values in new settings, to "sing unto the Lord a new song" in new situations. Through careful analysis of our own situations we must think creatively about how to infuse our economic environments with the sort of compassion that causes an upward lift for those who are weakest. We must think this through on all levels of economic life, from the political to the deeply personal. The text allows no compartmentalization between the Christian life and the economic identities we seek as societies and as people.

The Jubilee: Is God a Socialist?

Perhaps the most remarkable and controversial section of the Holiness Code is Leviticus 25, which (along with its counterpart in Deut 15) contains the requirements of the "jubilee." Many modern writers say that the jubilee supports modern socialism (or something very like it) and thus it exposes the great godlessness of Western capitalism.[10] The claim is most serious and has the advantage of appearing to take Scripture at its word, while defenders of the free market system often come off as dishonest and evasive in responding to the requirements of the jubilee. They commonly claim that the jubilee was never used, or that it is not relevant to modern economic systems.[11] But this will not do. As Jesus made clear, specific laws may pass away, but the universal truths embodied in them will not pass away, not a single "jot or tittle." A credible biblical theology of economic life must include a convincing account of the jubilee.[12]

Every fiftieth year was to be a year of jubilee, when all lands outside walled cities returned to the families that had first owned them.[13] On the day of atonement (note the context of worship), in the fiftieth year, a horn was to be blown in the land to "proclaim liberty . . . to all its inhabitants." The picture is powerful. Israel's great celebration of freedom from spiritual oppression was also a day of real-world economic restoration. When the horn blew, all Israel knew again that the realms of spirit and earth belonged together.

The explanation for this restoration of land is particularly important, because it gives the principles behind the jubilee that are the subject of intense debate. God speaks: "The land shall not be sold in perpetuity, for the land is mine; with me you are but aliens and tenants" (Lev 25:23).

Ronald Sider's interpretation is typical of a large trend in popular theology today. Although (unlike the more radical liberationists) he admits that Leviticus does not exactly *abolish* private property, he believes that it teaches a doctrine of "stewardship" that seriously weakens our modern Western tradition of property rights. The basic premise of this kind of stewardship is that, strictly speaking, we do not *own* property. Instead, we must realize that we are, in his words, "only stewards" of what *God* owns.[14] Sider thus believes that the jubilee (and all of Scripture) radically weakens our personal right to use and enjoy wealth. This weakened claim to ownership strengthens the rights of the community (church or nation) to establish systems that distribute wealth more evenly across the board to meet the basic "needs" of people.[15] Liberation theologians, too, judge that the jubilee warrants radical intervention into economic life by churches and governments to ensure the fair redistribution of property.

On the surface, this seems to be a reasonable argument. For the text does introduce a peculiar notion of property rights, and on that basis it does aim to liberate and restore people to the right quality of life through the compulsory redistribution of land. However, beyond this, the controlling values of the jubilee hardly resemble those of socialism or the even more moderate popular theories of stewardship. Rather, its ideas of justice, individual liberty, property rights and happiness are rooted in Israel's unique view of creation and thus are shaped by its special vision of flourishing, dominion and delight. This vision of life is not "capitalistic," but it has more in common with the spirit of modern democratic capitalism (rightly understood) than with the popular counterprograms.

First, the idea of equal distribution is alien to the moral conscience of the jubilee. The Promised Land simply was not divided equally among the tribes—the Levites got no land at all. The firstborn sons received twice the land given to the other sons (Deut 21:17). The daughters of Israel neither owned nor inherited anything. And non-Israelites had no share in the land. They could perhaps buy land and use it, but the jubilee would actually take it back from them and return it to the native owners.[16] And then there were the slaves. It is an intriguing irony that the same exodus that Gutiérrez and other liberation theologians herald as a "repudiation of slavery" and all social hierarchy also affirms the buying and selling of slaves (Lev 25:39-46).[17] Israelite slaves were released on the seventh year, and (provided they were male or married to a male Israelite who lived on the land) would have benefited from the jubilee. But non-Israelite slaves were neither released nor given a share in the restoration of land. Whatever the principle of redistribution was, it was certainly not an "egalitarian" one, that is, one that seeks an equal, or nearly equitable, distribution of property throughout the whole of society, with special regard for the most marginal persons.

Furthermore, the jubilee was not a utilitarian social program based on the model of stewardship that demands that each be given "according to his need." Many of the poorest people (aliens, sojourners, non-Israelite debtors and slaves) had no share in the land on the day of jubilee. Their economic need, however dire, played no role in the redistribution. It created no obligation for the rich to sacrifice their "luxuries" in order to serve the real needs of these poor. In fact, if a poor non-Israelite had managed to acquire land he would have lost it when the horn blew, because the mortgage returned to the native owners. In that instance, the land was released, and the industrious non-Israelite was disinherited (creating another inequality). The jubilee did nothing to restore such people. What it did was restore property and all its power to the old landed families, whether they needed it or not. Of course, if they had for some reason become poverty-stricken, the year of "release" would have released them from poverty. No doubt many would have sold their land precisely because they had come up short in their finances and needed to liquidate their capital to meet expenses. No doubt some had become impoverished in the most literal sense, and such people would have experienced the jubilee as the most basic kind of liberation from the pit of being poor. But the mere liberation of such people from poverty was not the explicit and driving logic of the jubilee. Its moral vision is greatly more complex than that.

Nor does the jubilee make relative the right of land ownership. In his classic study of Leviticus 25, Robert North opposed the more radical wing of Christian economic theory, which was then toying with communism as a biblical social system. North rightly wrote that the jubilee with its connected laws about economic life actually "stresses and safeguards the function of private property as an *incentive* to industrious energy."[18] According to North, the text itself is simply "untenable as a communist manifesto."[19] The strength of his argument is in a careful reading of the text itself. In fact, the text of Leviticus 25 not only affirms and safeguards the property rights of each tribe; it declares such rights to be unalienable, as unalterable and absolute as the God who gave it to them. In contrast to the way in which Sider and others interpret the concept of ownership, the text's logic is that *because* God owns the land and they are sojourners *with* God, the land cannot be sold in perpetuity. It must be with *them*, just as they must be with God. Their sojourn with the Lord has a place, a "religious space," and that place is the land.[20] This is the place in which they are made free to express their dignity and identity as God's own people. Thus the logic of the command is that the land cannot be taken from them, they cannot sell it in perpetuity and they are forbidden to share it, even in the charitable manner promoted by socialists and the more moderate Sider. As for Cain, to be banished from the land would be to be separated from the face of God, to be cast into the darkness of death.

God's ownership of the land does limit property rights, but not in the way that we might expect. It limits the property rights of non-Israelites or other buyers to a form of leasing, rental or temporary investment. Ironically, at the same time it limits the original property rights themselves to a state of absolute permanence. This creates a theocratic (God-ordained) idea of ownership that is stronger even than anything in our Western tradition of property rights. It more resembles what we find today in the Middle East, where Israelis and Arabs engage in a great struggle for possession of the Holy Land. Each side strengthens its claim to the land by asserting that *God* gave it to them, and that it thus *cannot* be sold in perpetuity, much less taken or given away.

Also, the property rights of the new owners are subordinated to higher obligations. But these are not the obligations of stewardship, as it is commonly understood. They do not weaken our grip on possessions in the context of ownership, which I think is the main intuition of stewardship, at least in popular Christian thought. On the contrary, they actually strengthen Israel's duty to maintain dominion over what God has entrusted to them. They are obligations to the stronger property rights of the Hebrews, the first owners, God's own people, who are to "sojourn" with him. To be a sojourner in this sense means to sojourn on the land. And it is not a weakened notion of property that guarantees the liberation of Israelites. On the contrary, it is this strengthened one. Because the land is God's, it is also *theirs* in perpetuity. It is thus an institutional repetition of the exodus for the people—an exodus that was grounded in and as solid as the earth itself.[21]

The best way to understand this vision is through the cross-reference to the theology of the land in the book of Exodus. In Exodus these two ideas are connected: God owns the earth, and Israel (if faithful and obedient) shall live a royal life of delight and dominion. In chapter 19 we read: "Indeed, the whole earth is mine" (note the claim of absolute ownership), "but you shall be for me a priestly kingdom and a holy nation" (Ex 19:5-6). The idea of God's absolute ownership generates the idea of Israel's royalty, proximity to God and special (holy) dominion on the earth. As the book of Revelation would later phrase it, God is shaping a "race of kings." Likewise, in Leviticus 25 the movement of the text is from sojourning with God in the land toward a life of abundance, not one of scarcity. "You shall observe my statutes and faithfully keep my ordinances, so that you may live on the land securely. The land will yield its fruit, and you will eat your fill" (Lev 25:18-19).

To put this vision in the context of economic systems, we note from the text that the morality of the jubilee must not be abstracted from the affirmations of banking, lending and general productivity at one's work that come through everywhere in these laws. The provisions for loans make little sense without an affirmative view of a moneyed financial system. The provisions for fairness in business ("You shall not cheat one another," Lev 25:14) make little sense apart from an affirmation of business and commercial enterprise. And the restoration of property was simply essential to the flourishing of the people. As I just stated, the whole point was a secure and abundant life. The purpose of the release was to protect the Israelite families from poverty and to empower them for both lives of redemptive action and delight in the abundance of the land. Having satisfied the moral conditions laid down by God, Israel would be satisfied in the physical realm. The words "the land will yield its fruit, and you will eat your fill" (Lev 25:19) summarize the entire jubilee vision. As noted earlier, eventually this broadens in diverse ways, throughout Scripture, to become the messianic vision for all human beings, and it ought to be at the core of our Christian vision today.

The division and subdivision of the land would also have created an intriguing political dynamic. By carving the political system into ever smaller (local and family-based) units of power, it would preserve a kind of democratic division of labor and a balance of power for individual families, empowering many more people, and it would reduce the risk of an oppressive, one-sided oligarchy or tyranny coming into existence. As North observes, "Lv 25 implies that the independent small property-owner is the backbone of a representative government."[22]

The exodus vision of Israel was indeed about economic liberation. But the basic unit of this liberation was *personal* liberty for most Israelites, including (as in the Garden of Eden) an invitation to dominate, cultivate and enjoy the fruits of the land.

In sum, the jubilee, in a new setting, expresses something very like the clustered theology of dominion, compassion and delight that we found in Genesis. In essence, it is creation theology. It contains that marriage of delight in abundance with the obligations that are born of true compassion and justice for others (although "others" had not yet broadened to include "all"). What the Garden, and later the land outside, was to Adam and Eve, the land of Palestine was to the people of ancient Israel. It was the sacred space in which their human dignity expressed itself. The text causes us to rethink the goodness of ownership under the right conditions. Fruitful property has the power to free us into the sacred space of the material realm, in which we can express our God-given dignity and identity as human beings. We ought not to think very long about the possible liberation of the poor apart from this affirmation of life and liberty through the possession of fruitful property.

The jubilee vision of the good life is indeed anchored by other conditions. It gives restrictions that impede our fallen, natural course toward licentiousness. Freedom to use and enjoy the land is good. The jubilee is a dramatic affirmation of this truth. The freedom to pursue life, liberty and property expressed God's vision of dominion and delight for his people. However, as we have seen in the other, connected laws, the system of freedom and delight was anchored by safeguards to protect everyone at least from the damaging effects of being poor. The jubilee protected the whole vision of delight for Israel, but the network of laws made sure that grace was extended, if not in equal measure, to those outside the dream. Not all in the land will know delight, but none ought to be poor beneath their dignity. For it is the just spirit of grace that animates the exodus vision of justice in the first place.[23]

On the whole, this interpretation of the jubilee makes its moral vision continuous with that of our forebears in modern democracy. Biblical scholar John Hartley sums up this point very well at the end of his long commentary on Leviticus 25.

> The Jubilee manifesto has not been lost on the pages of a forgotten OT book. It has had a leavening effect on social thought in the West, as the inscription of the words of v 10, "proclaim liberty throughout the land," on the Liberty Bell attests. This legislation . . . has contributed to the Western idea that every family has a right to own property. The view of land ownership herein, however, is revolutionary. . . . It promotes responsible work that attends ownership of property, and at the same time it promotes responsible brotherhood of all Yahweh's people arising from their faith in Yahweh. . . . This wonderful manifesto will continue to feed both the eschatological vision and utopian thinking until the kingdom of the Lord Jesus Christ is fully established.[24]

And it provides a vision for Christians today in which delight and dominion embrace in one moment with compassion and lives of justice, rightly imagined, for all human beings.

The Land: Where Delight and Compassion Embrace

It is a sad truth that in modern Christianity the theologies of dominion and delight are at war with the theologies of justice and compassion. But in the Old Testament, Israel was the land where delight and compassion embraced. A citation from Sider will help to illustrate the extent to which this aspect of Israel's economic vision can be misunderstood.

The law calls for one-tenth of all farm produce, whether animal, grain or wine, to be set aside as a tithe. "At the end of every three years you shall bring forth all the tithe of your produce in the same year; . . . and the Levite . . . and the sojourner, the fatherless, and the widow, who are within your towns, shall come and eat and be filled; that the LORD your God may bless you" (Deut 14:28-29).[25]

As Sider quotes the biblical text, it becomes almost solely a mandate for sacrificial compassion, a polemic against delight. In his reading, the tithe clearly demanded that Israel's productive class sacrifice the "extras" for the sake of the poor. The law of tithing is thus for him a text on "simpler living" for the poor's sake. (More radical demands would arrive with Jesus and the New Testament.) However, the completed reference to the command, in its context, gives a very different picture. Consider it at some length.

Set apart a tithe of all the yield of your seed that is brought in yearly from the field. In the presence of the LORD your God, in the place that he will choose, . . . you shall eat the tithe of your grain, your wine, and your oil, as well as the firstlings of your herd and flock, so that you may learn to fear the LORD your God always. But if, when the LORD your God has blessed you, the distance is so great that you are unable to transport it, . . . then you may turn it into money. With the money secure in hand, go to the place that the LORD your God will choose; spend the money for whatever you wish—oxen, sheep, wine, strong drink, or whatever you desire. And you shall eat there in the presence of the LORD your God, you and your household rejoicing together. As for the Levites resident in your towns, do not neglect them, because they have no allotment or inheritance with you.

Every third year you shall bring out the full tithe of your produce for that year, and store it within your towns; the Levites . . . as well as the resident aliens, the orphans, and the widows in your towns, may come and eat their fill so that the LORD your God may bless you in all the work that you undertake. (Deut 14:22-29)[26]

The complete citation unveils a text that is, surprisingly, first and foremost about delight and blessing in the bounty of the Lord's land. The tithe was for a feast of thanksgiving, a vast barbecue, with the finest meats, wines and beers that money could buy. "Whatever you desire" is the guiding voice, and this as the very expression of gratitude and service to God and other persons. This is not the theology of obligations, or of spare and "simpler" living, "scraping by for the kingdom," as one of my friends puts it. It is the theology of Eden, a theology that stems from an immodest passion for the good things of life. It is that "godly materialism" that we observed in the rooting soil of the creation story.

But the tithe is of course at the same time about grace and compassion. The spirit of celebration must be mindful of the Levite (Deut 14:27). Presumably, this meant inviting this family of priests, who had no land or inheritance, to the celebration. And at last, Deuteronomy requires that every *three* years the tithe must go to help the poor—but this is hardly the main point, as Sider suggests that it is. The vision rather is of a kind of delight that expresses itself in thanksgiving to God and with an eye on the poor. The land was the place where delight and compassion embraced.

The book of Deuteronomy gives a strong image of the material prosperity that came when Israel applied the right habits and systems to the land. Their destiny was not to go off "moderately ever after" into the wilderness to live on manna. God's aim was to bring them through the desert into a land "flowing with milk and honey." And this he did. He liberated them into a life of luxurious productivity and excess.

For the LORD your God is bringing you into a good land, a land with flowing streams, with springs and underground waters welling up in valleys and hills, a land of wheat and barley, of vines and fig trees and pomegranates, a land of olive trees and honey, a land where you may eat bread without scarcity, where you will lack nothing, a land whose stones are iron and from whose hills you may mine copper. You shall eat your fill and bless the LORD your God for the good land that he has given you. (Deut 8:7-10)

From the waters of chaos God had again created a good world. The text itself is overflowing with images of fertility and edenic good pleasure.

But there is also the other voice, the voice of deadly warning.

Take care that you do not forget the LORD your God, by failing to keep his commandments. . . . When you have eaten your fill and have built fine houses and live in them, and when your herds and flocks have multiplied, and your silver and gold is multiplied, and all that you have is multiplied, then do not exalt yourself, forgetting the LORD your God, who brought you out of the land of Egypt, out of the house of slavery. . . . Do not say to yourself, "My power and the might of my own hand have gotten me this wealth." But remember the LORD your God, for it is he who gives you power to get wealth. . . . If you do forget the LORD your God and follow other gods, . . . I solemnly warn you today that you shall surely perish. Like the nations that the LORD is destroying before you, so shall you perish, because you would not obey the voice of the LORD your God. (Deut 8:11-20)

To a people of dominion and delight, the Lord spoke of moral realities and dangers. As in Eden, where violation of the moral order meant death, so also in the land. Dominion and delight are powerful goods, but they are also gravely dangerous. The danger is a kind of hard arrogance and autonomy. This is the demonic spiritual energy that separates us from God, hardens us toward the poor and causes us to perish from the earth.

Nevertheless, the deadliest of dangers do not destroy the basic goodness of Israel's dominion and delight. Nor do the risks prevent the Lord from so blessing them with wealth. With right habits and institutions, delight and compassion can embrace in the human heart, and in whole societies.

Last Thoughts on the Exodus Vision

The God of the exodus is especially concerned with empowering the powerless, and so God's people must also be a people with a special regard for the poor. This is one of the abiding themes of Scripture, from beginning to end. The application is both to the heart and to the political process. On this all Christians should broadly agree. On the exact mechanisms for accomplishing that goal, Christians will no doubt disagree.

In my view, the exodus vision strongly encourages us to look elsewhere than to socialism or to current models of stewardship and "simpler living" for the best ideas. The exodus vision puts the many-faceted theology of Genesis into the shape of a holy nation. The "habits of heart" and the institutions of that nation were nourished by ideals of liberty, personal property and the life of dominion and delight—for God's people. This vision has great spiritual affinity with our modern democratic and capitalistic ideals (rightly understood), and with our image of "the good life" for *all* people.

The rich are not commanded to give the "extras" to the poor, but, from their position of power and blessing, they are required to nurture compassion in their hearts and so to institute laws that express the grace of God to the poor. Only a mood of honest realism about the brokenness of life makes possible the bond between power and compassion. Laws and social mechanisms are needed to restrain the darkness and to give light and hope to those who do not yet flourish. The prophets and books of wisdom will help us to expand and apply this vision in more personal terms.

5

THE PROPHETS
& WISDOM:
ECONOMIC LIFE IS
ETERNAL LIFE

We are what we eat.
LUDWIG FEUERBACH

Power is good, but it can turn deathly cold and dark. The film *Star Wars* brought this idea out in the mythic characters of Darth Vader and the evil Emperor. Human history has seen too many such players on its stage. Today's scandals in our own government have made the tabloids rich and a whole nation cynical about power. Lord Acton's adage that "power corrupts" today passes without argument.

This cynicism may be a sign of maturity in people who have been too optimistic and even naive about power, but it is not quite "Christian." The stories of creation and the exodus teach that, properly wedded with compassion, the positive power of dominion and delight is essentially good. Indeed it expresses our nature as human beings in the image and likeness of God. Nevertheless, the Bible, too, knows and warns about a negative power that brings chaos and destruction to the earth. The stories of creation and the exodus teach that powers of evil exist and have gained a foothold within us and in the world. We are "fallen," and the systems of the world are fallen.[1]

The writings of the prophets, especially, are about power in this negative form, about a demonic turning in the life of Israel. The little nation grew rich and powerful under its kings. But it also became, to use Yeats's phrase, "as pitiless as the sun." The land of delight and compassion, sadly, became a place of hardness and oppression.

The story of Israel's exile is a cruel reversal of the exodus. The ironies are themselves a lesson in humility. The very people God had freed from oppression became an oppressor. The people God had liberated from Egypt were thus sent back into slavery.

The story of the exile is also about wealth. A main reason for the exile was economic immorality. Israel's spiritual life had become rotten. But this was not expressed only mainly as a failure of pious religious observance. Israel's spiritual death was most clearly evident in the marketplace. More intensely than any group of writings in the Old Testament, the prophets teach that economic life is a measure and mirror of the soul. In that sense, economic life is eternal life. And (lest anyone be tempted to restrict the lesson to ancient Israel) the prophets apply this truth to the nations outside of Israel. They, too, stand before God, and he will judge them. He will judge their use of power and wealth, particularly as their policies (both domestic and foreign) touch the lives of the poor and powerless. The strong suggestion is that their message applies to all nations, especially those that have been blessed with power and wealth.

Amos: A Prophet to the Prosperous

The message of Amos came when times were good in Israel.[2] There was peace abroad and prosperity at home. Modern archaeology supports the general picture given by the book of Amos that it was a time of financial prosperity for the nation and, ironically, religion prospered.[3] Into this world of bright confidence walked the eerily stern figure of Amos. He saw his nation differently than it saw itself. Scholars agree that the message of Amos, while distinctive in several respects, is broadly representative of the latter prophets on the subject of economic life.[4]

Most of the prophetic books begin with oracles against Israel, and only then do they turn against the nations outside. In contrast Amos begins with a bitter judgment against the nations. Yet his approach is ironic: he has used this as a rhetorical device to set up the audience for a great fall. After finishing the last judgment against the nations, we can almost hear applause coming from Israel's corner, their pride as God's special people inflated to the maximum. At that very moment, however, Amos blasts them with accusations and judgments worse than anything he had addressed to the nations.

> Hear this word that the LORD has spoken against you, O people of Israel, against the whole family that I brought up out of the land of Egypt:
>
> You only have I known
> of all the families of the earth;
> therefore I will punish you
> for all your iniquities. (Amos 3:1-2)

This is the exodus vision in reverse. God liberated Israel from Egypt and made them the only people on earth that he has chosen. They are indeed his special people. *Therefore* God will punish them for their sins.

James Limburg suggests that "a pollster would have found a high degree of religious activity in the Israel of those days! But underneath it all, something was wrong."[5] Ron Sider is helpful in getting to the core of the problem:

> The explosive message of the prophets is that God destroyed Israel because of mistreatment of the poor. Idolatry, of course, was an equally prominent reason. Too often, however, we remember only

Israel's "spiritual" problem of idolatry and overlook the clear, startling biblical teaching that economic exploitation also sent the chosen people into captivity.[6]

Israel had reversed the moral energy of the exodus. They had twisted sacred life of liberation, dominion and delight into the way of the serpent. With compassion gone, delight in excess became ugly self-gratification. The majestic self became sated, harsh and full of narcissism. In short, the Israelites had become like their old captors, the Egyptians.

Amos describes two kinds of iniquity in Israel's economic life. The first is that people shamelessly exploited the weak simply to increase their own wealth.

They sell the righteous for silver,
  and the needy for a pair of sandals—
they who trample the head of the poor
  into the dust of the earth. (Amos 2:6-7)
They hate the one who reproves in the gate,
  and they abhor the one who speaks the truth.
Therefore because you trample on the poor
  and take from them levies of grain,
you have built houses of hewn stone,
  but you shall not live in them;
you have planted pleasant vineyards,
  but you shall not drink their wine. (Amos 5:10-11)

This cold, calculating oppression is obviously shameful. In fact, it is a safe bet that the majority of Israelites were horrified by it too. They (like most of us) did not see that the message applied to them. Most of them did not knowingly treat the poor like small prey. The prophet, however, does not let them (or us) off the hook so easily.

Amos saves his fiercest words for a second, more subtle evil. One of the harshest passages in the Bible is Amos's speech to the women of Israel, in the region of Bashan, who had built summer homes in the Samarian hills.

I will tear down the winter house
   as well as the summer house;
and the houses of ivory shall perish,
    and the great houses shall come to an end,
           says the LORD.
Hear this word, you cows of Bashan
   who are on Mount Samaria,
who oppress the poor, who crush the needy,
   who say to their husbands, "Bring something to drink!"
The Lord GOD has sworn by his holiness:
   The time is surely coming upon you,
when they shall take you away with hooks. . . .
Through breaches in the wall you shall leave,
   each one straight ahead. (Amos 3:15—4:3)

They oppress the poor, but how? Their evil is not direct—most of them probably never came into contact with the poor (except perhaps on the way to and from vacation homes). Is it that they had second homes in the mountains, or that they drank expensive wines?

   The rage of Amos burns again, later in the book:

Alas for those who lie on beds of ivory,
   and lounge on their couches,
and eat lambs from the flock,
   and calves from the stall;
who sing idle songs to the sound of the harp,
   and like David improvise on instruments of music;
who drink wine from bowls,
   and anoint themselves with the finest oils,
   but are not grieved over the ruin of Joseph!
Therefore they shall now be the first to go into exile,
   and the revelry of the loungers shall pass away. (Amos 6:4-7)

These texts help us to home in on the exact nature of the iniquities among the rich.

First, the moral judgment is not against enjoyment of fine things in a time of hunger. For then the prophecy must also be against David and against the whole vision of delight that God gave Israel in the first place. The evil is not simply in having ivory beds, eating good meat, drinking wine from bowls and being bathed in oils while others in the world starve. No, the message of Amos penetrates much more deeply to the bad spirit that infects these actions and makes them evil. For theirs is not the spirit of true dominion and delight, but of demonic narcissism and self-absorption.

It takes real depth, wisdom and spiritual discernment to know the difference between true delight and demonic narcissism. The prophet hears it in the music. He feels it in their manner of sleeping, eating and drinking. He sees it in their eyes and hears it in the shrill laughter, conversation and empty noises of the great, hollow houses. He smells it in the meats, wines and perfumes that they pour on themselves. But what exactly is it that the prophet senses?

Amos exposes the root of their evil when he says that they "do not grieve over the ruin of Joseph." Their whole spirituality expresses a lack of proper, sacred grief for the suffering around and about them. These are the leading figures of Israel. They identify themselves with the majestic power and glory of King David. But they know nothing of the passion and sacred grief for the nation and its poor to which his songs and music attest. They have lost touch with brokenness and thus have lost their own souls. Their celebrations have become frivolous, disgusting and pathetic displays of self-indulgence. Their music is nothing more than idle song.

I do not wish to say that the evil is only spiritual and not a matter of lifestyle. Had they truly grieved, perhaps there would have been no summer homes or beds of ivory. There most certainly would have been less lounging and lying around on them and more hours of work on solving national problems. The music no doubt would have become deeper and more powerful too. But Amos wisely does not fall into the trap of legalism, seeking to pinpoint the "politically correct" substance to use for bedmaking, or perhaps whether, in this world of need, beds might not be necessary at all. For the prophet, righteousness among the rich is not a matter of scraping away "luxuries" until a core of "necessities" has been reached. To such scraping there can be no satisfactory end, but only more scraping, and more guilt. No, it is a matter of finding one's true humanity. It is matter of becoming a mature person with a vision from the Lord and a heart for people, especially for the poor and powerless. The rich must be liberated, not from riches, but from the mind of the serpent. They must have the mind of God, the true Lord, who is their servant. They must strive toward the light of the exodus vision and recover the spirituality of redemptive power, which turns delight instantly to love. Amos prefigures the great saying of Jesus about the need for sacred grief in the joy of God's people: "Blessed are those who mourn."

Thus the Old Testament can both elevate the enjoyment of wealth to sacred status and lower it to a level beneath contempt. And thus we must try to understand the mystery and wonderful, blessed difficulty of being rich. Grieving is a key.

The Morality of Nations

Amos was not only interested in the morality of Israel, but also in that of surrounding nations. In the first two chapters, Amos delivers an attack on no less than six non-Israelite groups: Syria, Gaza (the Philistines), Tyre, Edom, the Ammonites and the Moabites. The crimes of these peoples were diverse, but all have one thing in common. They have all used their might to dominate other people in order to expand national power and wealth.

Damascus "threshed Giliad with threshing sledges of iron" (Amos 1:3). For hammering a weaker people like wheat into bits of grist, the power of Damascus will be broken, and "the people of [Syria] shall go into exile to Kir" (Amos 1:5).

Gaza "carried into exile entire communities, to hand them over to Edom" (Amos 1:6), invoking images of a gratuitous abduction for mere profit in the slave trade. For having done such a thing, God will punish them, and "the remnant of the Philistines shall perish" (Amos 1:8). The crime of Tyre was similar and the result just as bad (Amos 1:9-10).

And the Edomites? The crime was that "he pursued his brother with the sword and cast off all pity; he maintained his anger perpetually, and kept his wrath forever" (Amos 1:9). The image is of relentless, pitiless onslaught against a "brother," someone with whom one had made a pact or a covenant. Again, destruction is the consequence of breaking one's word.

At last, the Ammonites have "ripped open pregnant women in Gilead in order to enlarge their territory" (Amos 1:13). And the Moabites "burned . . . the bones of the king of Edom," that is, they desecrated a sacred burial site (Amos 2:1). Both are instances of brute insensitivity toward another, weaker people. Justice requires destruction of their strongholds by fire.

The logic of these moral judgments is familiar by now—it is the logic of the exodus. Those to whom God has given liberating power are now obligated to *be* a liberating power in the world. Using power for sheer self-interest is the very quintessence of national immorality. One of the most interesting passages in the Old Testament, Amos 9, shows how the exodus logic extends to all peoples that the Lord has blessed:

Are you not like the Ethiopians to me,
   O people of Israel? says the LORD.
Did I not bring Israel up from the land of Egypt,
   and the Philistines from Caphtor and the [Syrians] from Kir?
The eyes of the Lord GOD are upon the sinful kingdom,
   and I will destroy it from the face of the earth. (Amos 9:7-8)
Israel is not alone in having gone through an exodus; whether they

know it or not, other nations have been freed and empowered by the Lord. The Philistines and the Syrians are, in different ways, God's people and have received liberating power from his hand, although they are not expected to know or express it in the same way as are the Hebrews. This means that God does not judge and punish these nations arbitrarily. Judgment occurs within an active moral universe. The prophet appeals to their humanity, to their own desires and longings for liberation and delight. And he appeals to the fact that God has granted them these dreams. He implies that there is no good excuse for treating human beings in an inhuman manner. It is a living law of nature that we crave liberation and delight and, just as we crave these things for ourselves, we ought to crave them for everyone. If we are true to our own longings we will hate oppression wherever it exists, in whatever form. If we have received such power ourselves, and we use that power not to liberate but to oppress others, then we are on the way toward death as a people. God will act through forces of history to reverse the liberating energy, and he will send us back into the darkness. Israel will go back into slavery, Syria back to Kir, the Philistines into the abyss. Those in high places who abuse the weak and powerless will inevitably themselves be brought low. The message to the nations is that we live in a moral universe in which justice is required, and justice will be done.

Enthusiastic religion will not help:

I hate, I despise your festivals,
    and I take no delight in your solemn assemblies.
Even though you offer me your burnt offerings, . . .
    I will not accept them;
and the offerings of well-being of your fatted animals
    I will not look upon.
Take away from me the noise of your songs;
    I will not listen to the melody of your harps.
But let justice roll down like waters,

and righteousness like an everflowing stream. (Amos 5:21-24) Justice is in the essence of God, and it must be in the essence of God's people—both his special people *and* the peoples of the earth. Amos the prophet reminds us that righteousness is closely connected with societal justice. Righteousness and justice are not the same, but they are very closely related.[7] Justice is righteousness expressed in the social order. The prophet thus reminds us that the matter of national morality is not a marginal religious concern, but right at the center of what controls our future with God. The economic life of Israel and the nations cannot be untangled from the *eternal* lives of people.

The Wisdom Books: Will the Righteous Prosper?

The Wisdom books of the Old Testament—the Psalms, the book of Proverbs, Ecclesiastes and the book of Job—all probe the mysterious interaction between faith, morality and wealth. Since space permits only a summary, my focus will be on the book of Proverbs, which presents the worldview of biblical wisdom in a most interesting way. In addition, it gives special attention to the realm of economic life.[8] Proverbs especially provides a guiding vision of economic life for the people of God. I believe that this book can impart wisdom in areas where our understanding of the world is too simplistic. For instance, popular preachers today teach that true faith nearly always produces wealth, that wealth is a sure sign of God's blessing, and that poverty is punishment for evil. They claim that "God wants his people to prosper," and that "faith will bring material wealth." In spite of appeals to Proverbs for support, we shall see that biblical wisdom discourages us from picturing the moral world as this straightforward and predictable. There is a moment of truth in the popular preaching (which is usually neglected by its critics), but Proverbs helps us to see and appreciate the much greater complexity and mystery of moral life in the economic realm.

On the other hand, Proverbs can impart wisdom in areas where our understanding of the world has become too complicated and negative. For example, liberation theologians generally believe that the world system is so deeply corrupt that true righteousness normally results in poverty. Thus the poor are practically identical with the pious, the true people of God. Wealth in this world is normally the reward for compromise and compliance with oppressive powers. The general truth is that the wicked prosper, and the prosperous are the wicked. There is a moment of truth, too, in their appeal to the Wisdom books of the Old Testament for support. Nevertheless, we shall see that Proverbs keeps faith in the moral order and in human beings. It warns against simpleminded optimism, but it recovers something of the simplicity of childlike faith in God and the workings of his world.

It is true (and must be stressed) that Proverbs portrays being rich as good, and being poor as evil.

Wealth is a ransom for a person's life,

but the poor get no threats. (Prov 13:8)

The wealth of the rich is their fortress;

the poverty of the poor is their ruin. (Prov 10:15)

Thus, there is some truth in the popular preaching of "health and wealth." Critics who wish to correct the oversimplified view of the moral world often overlook this truth. Material wealth brings empowerment, strength and freedom. Poverty brings powerlessness, and leaves people trapped with no way out. These proverbs merely restate the biblical affirmation of dominion, delight and flourishing. True human life is not just rich in "spirit" but also in physical and material goods. On the reverse side, material poverty is an assault on the whole person, body and soul. Therefore, it is crucial to say that "God wants his people to prosper." Without this basic affirmation we weaken the whole Christian vision of dignity, worth and rights for people.

Other proverbs teach that our economic lives are wired to the moral order that God has established. Righteousness will have its reward, not only in heaven but on earth, and unrighteousness will end in material ruin. There is in fact a system of rewards and punishments, says Proverbs, and these include material gain and loss. Riches will be the direct reward for righteousness, and poverty the just consequence of irresponsible action (or inaction). For example:

The reward for humility and fear of the LORD
   is riches and honor and life. (Prov 22:4)
Whoever trusts in the LORD will be enriched. (Prov 28:25)
The appetite of the lazy craves, and gets nothing,
   while the appetite of the diligent is richly supplied. (Prov 13:4)
One who is slack in work
   is close kin to a vandal. (Prov 18:9)
A slack hand causes poverty. . . .
   A child who sleeps in harvest brings shame. (Prov 10:4-5)

These proverbs picture a moral universe that is operating as it should. The righteous prosper and the wicked perish. However, we must be very cautious in drawing conclusions from these proverbs. Does this ideal situation always exist, so that the claims of these proverbs are always true? Clearly not.

We must understand something about the nature of proverbs. Biblical scholar Raymond Van Leeuwen, in an article on wealth in Proverbs, points out that different proverbs often make contrasting points.[9] For example, Proverbs 26:4 says "Do not answer fools according to their folly." But in the next verse, we are advised to the contrary, "Answer fools according to their folly." What *does* Proverbs teach, then? Is it wise to answer the fool, or not? Van Leeuwen points out that it all depends on the situation. Proverbs is telling us that sometimes it is wise to answer a fool, sometimes it is not. It takes wisdom to know which proverb to apply in life. The wise person will know. Specific situations are attached to many proverbs, so that in that situation the proverb is true. But (as in the example of answering the fool) it may not be true in a different situation. Van Leeuwen writes: "We need to realize that proverbs are true *with regard to the particular situation they fit.* . . . What the German poet Goethe said of languages is better said of proverbs: 'He who knows one, knows none.' "[10]

Sometimes the world works according to clear justice. In those situations, the proverbs above are true, and they declare those situations good. In those situations the righteous are the rich; God identifies with them and they with him. The wicked are the poor, and God does not identify with them.

However, ancient Israel found out the hard way that the world does not always operate by straight justice. Anyone who thinks that it does is in danger of severe disillusionment and disappointment with God. I have known many students and colleagues who have lost faith in God altogether because their simplistic understanding and false expectations made it impossible to cope with the hard realities of life. The rain will fall on the just and the unjust. So will the death winds of hurricanes, the quaking of the earth, the random evils of disease and death. Suddenly, the ordered, predictable world comes apart and it seems that there is no order, and no God behind it. The whole book of Job puts in dramatic form this realization that terrible poverty may come on even the most righteous person for no visibly good reason.

Biblical wisdom stresses that we cannot predict with certainty that faith will bring material flourishing and delight. Nor may we say with confidence that unrighteousness will always be punished by poverty. In fact, Ecclesiastes says that he has seen "righteous people who perish in their righteousness, and there are wicked people who prolong their life in their evil-doing" (Eccles 7:15). Besides the book of Job, many of the Psalms are soul-bent, lyrical questions put to music and sung to God, begging him for an explanation of such injustices, and pleading for true justice to come. The book of Ecclesiastes presses the outer boundaries of melancholy to find gladness of heart, not through shallow optimism, but through grim sadness. "The heart of the wise is in the house of mourning" (Eccles 7:4). The truth is that the righteous often suffer while the wicked prosper.

Contrary to the above proverbs (and to much popular Christian preaching), in this world wickedness too often pays. Proverbs admits what television character J. R. Ewing explained as the key to his success: "Once you forget integrity, the rest is easy." The wicked prosper so often that we are tempted to form a new rule of cause and effect. If you are unrighteous you will get rich. And as the wicked prosper, people of integrity are often broken and poor. In fact (contrary to the other proverbs), their faith and integrity actually cause their poverty!

Job is a stunning example of this upside-down world. To the simple minds of his "comforters" Job appears certainly to be an unrighteous man. Otherwise he would not be suffering ruin. But this is false. The book condemns them for this terribly wrong judgment. God exposes their righteous certainty for what it is—smug, pious arrogance about the predictability of life and God. In Job, the real truth is that the normal rules have been shattered into a thousand pieces. Their rigid assumptions made them blind to the truth. In their good fortune, in the absence of conspicuous evil on Job's part, theirs was not to preach, pontificate or judge, but to show compassion. God alone sees to the essence of moral situations. Ours is not to judge in any final sense, but to act in humility and love toward the fallen. "The rest," to quote from Eliot, "is not our business." In such cases, the presumption of grace should be with the poor. God will take care of the rest.

Several "better-than" sayings probe this strange injustice and inspire us not to lose moral courage, if we ourselves suffer wrongly.

Better is a little with righteousness
　　than large income with injustice. (Prov 16:8)
Better is a little with the fear of the LORD
　　than great treasure and trouble with it.
Better is a dinner of vegetables where love is
　　than a fatted ox and hatred with it. (Prov 15:16-17)
Better to be poor and walk in integrity
　　than to be crooked in one's ways even though rich. (Prov 28:6)

Here is the solemn moment of truth in liberation theology. Circumstances may be so deeply fallen that virtue becomes evil, and vice versa. As in Yeats's poem, all values are turned around, "the falcon cannot hear the falconer." To be righteous leads to ruin, and to be unrighteous brings riches. In such situations God is with the poor, and against the rich. He is with the poor, though, not because they are poor but because they have kept their integrity and suffer for it. They are what the Psalms refer to as the 'anawîm, the righteous poor, who are God's true people even though they appear to be abandoned and lost. In truth, God has not abandoned the righteous poor. They are his people in a very special sense. They are "better off," "richer" than the unrighteous who are rich. This is the proper context for saying that God identifies with the poor. In the real world, moral lines are not easily drawn—God identifies with neither the rich nor the poor apart from moral situations in real life.

We draw moral courage from knowing that justice will prevail. Unlike Woody Allen's *Crimes and Misdemeanors*, wisdom teaches that the dust of death will one day come to powerful, hollow people.

> The getting of treasures by a lying tongue
>> is a fleeting vapor and a snare of death. (Prov 21:6)
> Treasures gained by wickedness do not profit,
>> but righteousness delivers from death. (Prov 10:2)

The truth is that the wicked do not really prosper; they only seem to. Righteousness will prosper and unrighteousness will be ruined. Without fully picturing an afterlife, or being specific about the timing of justice, Proverbs envisions a truly just outcome for God's people.

> The faithful will abound with blessings,
>> but one who is in a hurry to be rich will not go unpunished.
>> (Prov 28:20)
> The violence of the wicked will sweep them away,
>> because they refuse to do what is just. (Prov 21:7)

There is, then, a moral order of cause and effect in God's universe.

However, we must understand this order in "the long run." Not every evil is punished immediately, nor every good rewarded. The existence of a just moral order is a matter of faith, not straightforward observation. God's execution of justice is more art than science. Like Abraham and Job, we must trust that the Judge of all the earth will do right. The Lord brings justice from painfully long processes of history. He creates his tapestry from endless threads in countless times and places. The God of Scripture is much slower to judge or act than are the preachers of either popular or liberation theology. Nevertheless, wisdom teaches that, in the end, "all manner of thing will be well," as T. S. Eliot wrote. Not *every* time and circumstance will be just, but, in the end, *all* of time will be just.

Proverbs obviously modifies the popular theology that marks the rich in this life as God's true people. But it also challenges the more academic habit of identifying them hastily as the poor. Proverbs does not praise or condemn either the poor or the rich as economic classes of people. Nor does it establish a pattern that would justify thinking in simplistic terms one way or the other. Nor does it establish a fixed law of expectations for God's people. If we are faithful, we should not *expect* to become rich, although we might; nor should we assume that poverty and suffering are always the badge of righteousness, although they might be. In such times we must take heart. Economic life in the fallen world is very complex, and many outcomes are possible. Wisdom is the key. As is proper vision. This we do know: God's ideal vision for his people is that coupling of power with compassion.

> Those who mock the poor insult their Maker;
> > those who are glad at calamity will not go unpunished.
> (Prov 17:5)

In contrast, the rich person who helps the poor is thereby blessed.

> Whoever is kind to the poor lends to the LORD,
> > and will be repaid in full. (Prov 19:17)
> Those who are generous are blessed,

for they share their bread with the poor. (Prov 22:9)
  One who augments wealth by exorbitant interest
  gathers it for another who is kind to the poor. (Prov 28:8)
The rich person who empowers the poor through the use of financial leverage "lends to the Lord," that is, is doing the Lord's work. Such a person is acting in a godly manner, expressing the identity of God the liberator of the oppressed. If it is true to say that God identifies with the righteous poor, it is also true that the righteous rich, who show grace to the poor, identify with God, and God thus identifies with them. And at one point Proverbs reminds us that either wealth or poverty can lead to evil:

  Give me neither poverty nor riches; . . .
  or I shall be full, and deny you,
    and say, "Who is the LORD?"
  or I shall be poor, and steal,
    and profane the name of my God. (Prov 30:8-9)
Perhaps that is the appropriate prayer for most of us. Proverbs thus carves its vision of economic life in God's moral universe. Our study of this vision in the Old Testament should help to broaden and deepen our grasp of things in the New Testament. We are now ready to take this crucial step in our exploration.

6

THE SOCIAL
& ECONOMIC
STANDING
OF JESUS

Is not this the carpenter, the son of Mary?
MARK 6:3

Most of us learned something in our church upbringing about the "person and works" of Jesus Christ. We know that Jesus was both man and God, that he died for our sins, that he was raised from the dead and that he will come again to judge the world. Also (with some help from picture books), many of us grew up imagining Jesus as a rather harmless person, a kind and gentle man who went around doing good. I recall wondering, as a boy, how such a person could have any enemies at all, let alone have something so awful as crucifixion happen to him.

Theologians have recently unearthed some things about Jesus that have come as a shock to people who were raised on the "gentle Jesus" of popular church convention.[1] Liberation theologians, especially, have shown that the Jesus of the Gospels was revolutionary and dangerous. Indeed, from one point of view, Jesus was a constant threat to the centers of power. He provoked their fury, and they rose against him.

What was so revolutionary and dangerous about Jesus? To liberation theologians the whole "Christ event" was like a concentrated form of the exodus. Jesus Christ united and "identified" himself with the poor and powerless of the earth, against the rich and powerful. Jesus' whole life and all of his teachings expressed this revolutionary bond between God and the poor in their struggle against the vast beast of world power.

Christians need to hear that Jesus unleashed revolution throughout the whole cosmos, in heaven and on earth.[2] This revolution comprehends all of life—our bodies, minds and souls, the world and its systems. As theologian Abraham Kuyper wrote, there is not a single square inch of the universe about which Christ does not say, "This is mine." And we do need to hear that Jesus had a special mission to the people whom the world wished to forget. The Son of the exodus God will not let them be forgotten. He will not let us forget them without also forgetting him.

But there is still much to debate. In many groups, it is a matter of "theological correctness" that Jesus "identified" with the poor. It passes without question that he was born and grew up in poverty, that his followers were mainly poor people, that together they adopted lives of poverty during their public mission, and that his primary audience was the poor multitudes. Coupled with this picture of his life is a radical interpretation of his teachings. We commonly hear it stressed that Jesus condemned the rich and blessed the poor. This portrait of Jesus is a powerful influence in the Christian political world today. Whole lives and communities have been built around it. However, I have come to believe that it is a poor reflection of reality. And in spite of the good it has done, it misleads people at very crucial points in forming their Christian economic vision.

In this chapter I shall seek to picture Jesus and his nearest followers as economic persons in their own world. It may at first seem strange, but research into that setting shows clearly enough that Jesus, the Twelve and his larger circle of followers did not come from the really poor sectors of society. They came mainly out of small businesses and trades that belonged to something like the Palestinian "middle class"—to help picture it in our terms. The main purpose of this chapter is to show that this was so, and to ponder what it means for Christian theology and life. Later chapters shall examine the lifestyle of Jesus and his disciples during their public mission, and then the detailed teachings of Jesus on riches.

The Social and Economic World of Jesus

In order to comprehend the economic identity of Jesus Christ, we must try to gain an accurate picture of the world around him. Jesus was born into an unstable political climate. Israel was an unwilling member of the vast Roman Empire. By all recent accounts, the young Jesus grew to adulthood in a society that was highly stratified and marked by extremes of wealth and poverty.[3] Recent studies show that Israel had become a rumbling volcano that threatened to erupt into violence at any moment. Mobs of peasants hungered and thirsted for justice.[4] Riots would break out without warning. The Romans reacted by positioning a small army in the major centers to help the Jewish authorities to police them. To orthodox Jews this cooperation symbolized the worst possible form of compromise—very like what a Western presence in the Middle East means to zealous Arabs today.

The poor of Jesus' Palestine were many. Worst off were the homeless, the thousands of beggars who tried to survive on the streets. Often such people were disabled—blind, lame, riddled with disease, wretched in every respect. There were also street children—we do not know how many—orphaned and abandoned to the savaging chaos of life. However, the multitudes of poor people had some relief. The "poor tax" was still in use, which meant that every third year the annual tithe would be distributed among the poor. The gleaning laws were also in effect in Jesus' day.[5] Further, the poor received help from almsgiving, various charities and a welfare system that grew from the synagogue. This last system may have influenced the early church as described in Acts.[6] But this help was just a drop in the bucket. The poorest of the poor were horribly oppressed. In all likelihood the multitudes who flocked to Jesus came mainly from this downtrodden mass of suffering people (more on this later).

A different kind of poverty afflicted the "working poor." Among these were day-laborers and slaves. The Roman Empire was full of slaves, even in Israel, although not as many were there as in the Gentile regions. Most were domestic servants in the wealthiest homes.[7] Matthew's picture of day-laborers (Mt 20:2, 9) sitting in the marketplace waiting for work also is true to the situation as best we know it.[8] Neither group earned much beyond its "daily bread." Day-laborers depended entirely on day-to-day contracts. Often they had no real estate or inheritance to fall back on and, even if they managed to get by, had little security in their lives. They were poor by any standard.

Another group of working poor were the so-called *am haaretz*, "the people of the land." Jewish peasants were in some respects the life-blood of the economy. But research indicates that the system was against them. In Israel the powerful families used land as a political weapon. This maneuvering naturally benefited the largest land holders and usually hurt the peasants. Sudden land liquidations or controlled changes in the markets worked against the smaller land-owners.[9] It was not unusual for desperate peasants to sell what little land they owned to pay off debts. And to be landless in a landed economy was to be powerless. It seems that the jubilee must not have been in force.

The entire atmosphere, which the Romans had set up to maintain stability, guaranteed a high level of resentment among the people, and the option of joining a patriotic band of robbers or guerrilla fighters (sometimes called zealots) became attractive to more than a few. Such was the world into which Jesus came preaching and teaching that the kingdom of God was at hand. No wonder many mistakenly understood him to speak of an immediate political revolt against Rome and their collaborators.

At the other extreme were the rich, and in Palestine the rich were very often (though not always) people who had sold out to Rome. To pious Jews they epitomized the "unrighteous rich" of Old Testament religion. Traitors to everything sacred, thus they prospered. At the top was the royal family of the hated Herod. His ruthlessness and political cunning were as legendary as they were profitable.[10] One of Herod's favorite ploys was to take land from the people whom he distrusted and give it to proven loyalists. To these belonged the holy priesthood and all the riches that went with it, including revenues from taxation and a corner on all sorts of markets connected with the religious life of the nation.[11] Needless to say, they did not enjoy the love of the people. We will comprehend the New Testament better if we understand that financial advantage in Israel often implied direct involvement with political evil and injustice.

Tax collectors, of which there were at least three sorts, rated high on the scale of unrighteousness. The most powerful—and most hated—were the publicans. These were large-scale "tax farmers" who were "infamous for their fortune and fraud in the late Republican period of Roman imperialism."[12] We can perhaps picture them as supervisors atop a large pyramid system of toll collectors. In the Roman Empire tax collecting was a kind of investment business done under contract with private citizens who agreed to pay the sum of the tax due from conquered territories to the government. They were then free to collect the money from the territories in any way they saw fit, and to do so at a profit![13] They thus employed a staff of people whose job was to exact as much money from the people as they could to repay the investment at risk. In charge at the local level were "chief tax collectors" (such as Zacchaeus in Lk 19:2-9), powerful middlemen in the system.[14] Obviously, their economic level was high, but their social status was near the bottom of the scale. Likewise was the situation of the smaller collectors beneath them who set up toll booths and operated as businesses in smaller localities. Jesus' disciple, Levi (or Matthew as he came to be called), was perhaps one of these third-level operators. No doubt some tax collectors were fairer, and hated less, than others.[15] But the New Testament claim that tax collectors were among the most active followers of Jesus, and that one of them even became a member of "the twelve," is truly astonishing if we think that Jesus was essentially a man of the righteous poor who opposed the unrighteous rich.[16]

The polarized political and economic situation made the moral extremes worse. It was difficult to be rich in that environment without being corrupt, and it was a natural path from integrity to rags. Still, some of the recent studies exaggerate the scene. The histories give glimpses of rich people who were also good and poor people who were not. In time, we shall see how Jesus responded to them.

These standard social studies are helpful, but they do tend to over-dramatize things. The peasantry was not always on the losing end.[17] On the local level, success in the markets was often related more to the quality of one's produce; and sometimes the manipulated inflation (price-fixing) by the rich actually created better prices for the poorer landowners.[18] Furthermore, between the extremes of wealth and poverty was a kind of middle class, for lack of a better term, that was very important. Ancient Palestine "possessed all the craftsmen, specialized workers and performers of simple manual tasks possessed by any other normal economy of the ancient world."[19] The economy was strong enough to be differentiated and to support a high degree of specialization. The abundance of crafts and special industries indicates a lively circulation of goods. The rural areas most typically produced pottery, silk and other services connected with the fishing industry (particularly in Galilee).[20] Wine, oil and perfumes also came from various locales. Almost all Jewish clothing was made in Palestine and commerce surrounding wool was very vital to economic movement.

Craftsmen of all kinds lived throughout Israel. Naturally, the majority operated in Jerusalem and the other cities, but they also worked in the smaller towns and villages. The list of trades is long: the making of handicrafts, leatherwork, rope, baskets and basalt millstones, special stones for burial and mason stones for building (perhaps Jesus' special skill)[21]—all occurred in rural regions. There were also metal workers and bakers (who had organized their own guild), butchers, incense specialists, money-changers, traders of various kinds and bankers. The temple alone supported an economy that employed around twenty thousand people. There were weavers, cheesemakers, woolcombers, coppersmiths and cobblers.[22]

Jesus the Carpenter: His Incarnation and Identity

This picture of ancient Palestine helps to sharpen our questions and answers about the social and economic identity of Jesus before his public mission. It also helps us to put the more radical, popular interpretation into perspective. Ronald Sider, for example, describes Jesus' identity this way:

> He was born in a small, insignificant province of the Roman Empire. His first visitors, the shepherds, were persons viewed by Jewish society as thieves. His parents were too poor to bring the normal offering for purification. Instead of a lamb, they brought two pigeons to the Temple. . . . Jesus was a refugee and then an immigrant in Galilee. . . . Since Jewish rabbis received no regular fees for their teaching, Jesus had no regular income during his public ministry. (Scholars belonged to the poorer classes in Judaism.) Nor did he have a home of his own. . . . He sent his disciples in extreme poverty.[23]

This view of Jesus as poor in the whole manner of his life generates a system of social values and a kind of spirituality:

Only as we feel the presence of the incarnate God in the form of a poor Galilean can we begin to understand his words: "I was hungry and you gave me food, I was thirsty and you gave me drink. . . . I was naked and you clothed me. . . . Truly, I say to you, as you did it to the least of these my brethren, you did it to me" (Mt 25:35-36, 40).[24]

Now it is true that Jesus did not enter this world with great power and glory. As Paul wrote, he "emptied himself, taking the form of a slave" (Phil 2:7). And "though he was rich, yet for your sakes he became poor" (2 Cor 8:9). There is indeed an awesome lowliness about the entire incarnation. There is terrible downward movement from divine glory to human form, and in human form a descent, through the cross, into hell itself. Author and poet John G. Neihardt called this "the pity of the manger"—the king of the universe bundled in rags, sleeping in a dirty wooden feed trough inside a cow barn. It is the might of Mary's Magnificat in Luke's Gospel. The Lord of glory is a God who "has scattered the proud," who "has brought down the powerful from their thrones, and lifted up the lowly." He is a God who "has filled the hungry with good things, and sent the rich away empty" (Lk 1:46-56). A young girl from Nazareth with no prestige and a young man who had only enough money at the time (perhaps because the pregnancy appeared obviously illegitimate and the dowry was denied by Jewish law) to buy the poorest offering of sacrifice to dedicate their son were the mother and father of the king.

But we must be very careful not to romanticize the event by reducing its spirit of humility and lowliness to one of literal *economic* poverty. The character of the event is far more inclusive than Sider's description suggests. Not only were the poor shepherds called; the rich astrologers, the Magi from the East, saw Jesus' highness in the stars and came to worship him. They brought precious gifts of gold, frankincense and myrrh (that would have greatly helped the young family in exile and afterward). It is true that the little family fled into Egypt. But it has seldom been noticed or stressed that, before they returned to Galilee, they somehow managed to obtain housing in Bethlehem, and they apparently lived there for three years, until Herod had done his worst (Mt 2:11). And when they returned to Nazareth they were not "immigrants," as Sider calls them, but local residents returning home with resources enough to start, or rejoin, a family business.

We must also avoid exporting our modern economic labels into the world of Jesus, although some of this is unavoidable. He might have been judged "poor" by modern American standards, but no one in his own culture would have classified him that way. Until he was about thirty, Jesus worked in Nazareth as the son of a carpenter, as tradition translates it. He was a *tektōn*, or "builder." The absence of Joseph suggests that his eldest son had inherited the business. That is how he was known in his hometown, as Jesus "the builder" (Mk 6:3).[25]

Jesus worked for most of his life at this trade. That is why New Testament experts Walter Pilgrim and Martin Hengel both judge that Jesus did not grow up in poverty, but belonged to the middle class of his day. According to Pilgrim, "If the tradition that Joseph was a carpenter carries historical veracity, as we have no reason to doubt, then Jesus' family actually belonged to the middle structure of his society, to the small traders and artisans."[26] Hengel states:

> We should note first that Jesus himself did not come from the proletariet of day-labourers and landless tenants, but from the middle class of Galilee, the skilled workers. Like his father, he was an artisan, a *tektōn*, a Greek word which means mason, carpenter, cartwright and joiner all rolled up into one (Mark 6:3).[27]

We have no detailed ledger of Jesus' business, no yearly tax statements or the like. We know nothing about his income or personal habits of investment, savings, charity and so forth. It seems clear, though, that the business supported a reasonably large family. A builder's son in

Nazareth may not have been rich, but he would have had much to be thankful for compared with the majority of the population.[28] And there is good reason to believe that builders in the region prospered during those years. They had all the work they could handle because of massive construction that went on in nearby Sepphorus.[29] This important city had been destroyed when a rebellion broke out there on the occasion of Herod's death in 4 B.C. His son, Herod Antipas, also a great builder, had the whole city rebuilt, making it an "ornament of Galilee" and bringing it into the orbit of Roman rule during Jesus' lifetime.[30] If Jesus worked in this system, as is likely, he not only prospered but was implicated directly in the political workings of the Herodian dynasty.

Jesus was not socially poor either. He may not have been a prince or a member of the elite, but he did not grow up, as many children did, homeless and hellbound on the streets of the inner city. Social status is in some ways a better measure of wealth in ancient society than is money, and his was pretty high. To call him a "poor Galilean," as if to suggest that he was somehow disadvantaged, misses the mark.

Studies have shown that Nazareth was a small Jewish town, but, as Batey and other recent sources show, it was no backwater.[31] Trade routes connected the cities of Galilee with the Greek cities of the coastal plain, and Nazareth was also connected geographically (by valley) to the Mediterranean Sea. All the towns in the region where Jesus was located "were Greek-speaking and cosmopolitan, located on busy trade routes connected to Roman administrative centers."[32]

And in the environment of Nazareth Jesus would have had many advantages. He was first of all Jewish, and he was a firstborn male in a family with a reputable home and business. This guaranteed an education, an inheritance and many other privileges that most of his contemporaries did not have. He seems to have been strong, wise and well respected (Lk 2:40). Luke's statement that the young Jesus "increased . . . in divine and human favor" (Lk 2:52) comports with our image of him reading the sacred scroll in the synagogue. Some may have been suspicious about his origins, especially as Mark records the crowd's reaction to him: "Is not this the carpenter, the son of Mary [rather than of Joseph] and brother of James and Joses and Judas and Simon, and are not his sisters here with us?" (Mk 6:3). But surely the incredulousness about his implied claims was more due to their mundane familiarity with Jesus than to a long background of ostracism. Hometown carpenters do not quite conform to our image of the ideal messianic prince! Nevertheless, in his economic and social conditions, growing up, there was much that others in his day and age could envy.

The Incarnation and the Economic Person of Jesus
Orthodox Christians believe that Jesus' life was not merely a human event. We believe that it was an *incarnation*—the birth of the divine Son of God into the world. To me this means that his social and economic identity was not an accident, as it perhaps is for ordinary humans. Liberation theologians are right—unlike ordinary humans, Jesus deliberately chose his social identity. His choice expresses something of his character, the character of God. And it expresses something about the character of his life as a human person in the world of culture. It says something about God's identity and about his identification with humanity, about that with which God, in Jesus, has identified himself. But God's identity and his social and economic identification are far broader and more inclusive than what liberation theologians suggest.

Jesus' chosen identity as part of a construction business, centered in Nazareth, in Galilee, sharpens our vision of God and how he has identified with human beings. In chapter one I described the student who was ashamed of himself for being middle class. He was ashamed to be sheltered by his upbringing from the evils of the world. He was ashamed to have been privileged to enjoy good things while others suffered. His teachers urged him to think this way. They seemed to believe that almost nothing was further from the spirit of Jesus than the American middle class. But the incarnation story suggests otherwise. It shows that there is something right and good about growing up in a healthy environment. If God had used the moral reasoning of some theologians today, Jesus would have been born in the inner city of Jerusalem. He would have grown up among the hordes of beggars, prostitutes, street-children, criminals and worse. He would have been the (probably female) child of a single-parent household. Or he would have been a landless peasant, bred on social rage and resentment toward authority and power. Then he truly would have identified himself with the really poor. But he did not. The loving heavenly Father took care that his Son had an environment where he "became strong" and was "filled with wisdom" (Lk 2:40).

I shall later explore Jesus' life, ministry and teachings, and discuss his commitment to the poor, but we must first know that in the incarnation God has identified with innocence and stability and with a vision of personhood that is not entirely unlike what many of us seek in life for ourselves and our children. People who came from such a background—persons like Peter, James, John, Joanna and others not named—were rich in potential to serve in the kingdom of God. Perhaps that is why Jesus identified initially with them, and they with him.

There is also a point to be made about work and vocation. Jesus' chosen (if we believe in the incarnation) place in his society as a tradesman reflects a certain *goodness* on property, on creative, productive work and on the sort of personhood that goes with it. Remembering the Bible's theology of creation, it is interesting that Christ somewhat was more closely tied to the cultural system of the city, fathered by Cain, than he was to the land.[33] The commercial system is thus, in a way, redeemed through his economic person. Although most of his teaching metaphors came from the agricultural world, the New Adam himself worked at a productive trade within the economic system of Israel in the Roman Empire. He was a builder and a businessman, and this was apparently part of what expressed his perfection as a human being. This point needs to be made, partly because the simple goodness and diginity of trade and business, and the personhood that comes with such a life, are not always appreciated by moral theologians and churchmen of our day.

This last point is connected with a third one. Many Christians, like my student, are confused on the matter of involvement in a fallen world. The incarnation of Jesus, especially if we accept his involvement in the work of rebuilding Sepphorus (and even if not), means that his identity was deeply interwoven with the political and economic system of Rome. He became an economic person within the moral conditions of that historical web-work. This is relevant to a line of thinking about "structural evil" that has become very influential today. Ron Sider has helped to spread the view among Christians that "structural evil" is morally indistinguishable from "personal evil." His point is that we are morally responsible, not just for our own actions but for our *involvement* in world systems and for the moral actions of countless others. For example, he argues that people who live upright personal lives, but then do things like hold "stock in companies that exploit the poor of the earth," are still reprehensible.[34] No matter how good their personal lives, such people are implicated in the moral evil of the systems that benefit them. According to Sider, "if one is a member of a privileged class that profits from structural evil, and if one does nothing to try to change things, he or she stands guilty before God."[35]

Anyone who thinks about this for a very long time will understand that it is a serious and sweeping charge. It is serious because it implies not only that we work within systems that are *fallen* but that (unless we make the needed efforts to change) working in a fallen system is *sinful*. It makes us guilty before God. And it is sweeping because it would finally seem to cast the net of guilt over everyone who is at all involved in the world, even those who "try to change things." Unless we live on desert islands (and perhaps even if we do), I believe it is true that we all profit to one degree or another from sinful systems—without trying to change them. Most often we do not try to change the offending structures because we do not know about them. Usually we have no way to know about them. The global world system is so vast and complex that we would have to be nearly omniscient to know even a slice of the fallenness that we "profit" from. The more involved in the world we are, the less our ability to know, much less to "try to change," the relevant evil structures in any manner significant enough to merit the claim that we have. By this way of reasoning, the greater our involvement is in the world, the greater will be our guilt before God. And I pass over the futility of trying to change, as Sider puts it, even the thin slice that we do know. For once we start down the track of uncovering "structural evils" that we "profit" from (especially if we are good at this sort of analysis), there is of that uncovering no end. The "damned spot" remains.

Leave it to say that the principle of "guilt by implication" makes futile any attempt to be involved in the world with integrity. Either we must be involved without integrity, in a state of perpetual guilt (which is no option for the Christian), or we must seek to escape from the fallen system itself as completely as we can. Thus, this principle, given by Sider (and others) as a means of transforming society, is really a moral prohibition against working within the fallen world—it is a counsel of separatism. In fact it requires significant withdrawal from the very system it wishes to reform.

Fortunately, we do not have to prove this last point at great length.[36] The principle of "guilt by implication" is not just a recipe for futility and withdrawal from the world. It is a wrongheaded reading of Scripture, especially where its ideas of sinfulness and guilt are shaped by comparison with the identity and life of Jesus Christ. He is the Christian standard.

But as we have seen, Jesus was himself privileged to a certain extent, and he clearly profited (perhaps greatly) from the Roman economic system. Like all Jews, in spite of the disadvantages of subjection to Roman might, he benefited from the stability of peace, legal order, good road systems, stimulated cash flow and building projects (not least in Sepphorus) that improved standards in his own region, and a long list of things that (often through Rome's puppet Herod) made life in the region better. But the "structures" of evil included totalitarian dictatorship, gratuitous military conquest, slave labor, unfair taxation, the expedient use of genocide and a thousand other things that would (rightly) horrify the modern moral conscience of reforming theologians. Because Jesus was a true human being who lived and worked within that economic system, it was simply impossible that he not profit from very great structural evils. And so far as we know he did nothing directly to change them. He did not speak out against them even when he had opportunities to do so. Only a complete reconstruction of the history could obscure the Gospels' unanimous telling that their Lord was loath to present his kingdom as a worldly counterforce to the rule of Rome. This seems to have been an outrage to his more puritanical contemporaries, who thought him careless about his contacts with people such as Roman soldiers, tax collectors and others who typified cultural godlessness. But this did not move him much. Instead, he condemned *them* for their lack of grace toward the human condition.

The principle of "guilt by implication" is so relentless, rigid and unforgiving, then, that not even Jesus can pass its tests for goodness. It makes him, too, sinful and guilty for his manner of involvement in the world. This should be enough to discredit it as a Christian way of working out our economic lives. We can be liberated, at least, from the sorts of obligations that it lays on us. Our form of work in the world, including our righteous protests against the evils within it, must take another moral shape, one that is far less limited in terms of what

Christians may, or may not, engage in vocationally.

Christians must live lives that protest against evil and injustice. It may well be argued that Jesus' whole public mission was a kind of cosmic overturning of dark principalities and powers.[37] But the issue of vocation is very complex. Of course there are systems that are essentially evil in ways that make our involvement in them wrong (selling drugs, prostitution, pornography and the like). And there may be professions that our personal sense of conscience will not allow us to make our vocations. This could be overscrupulousness on our part, or it could be the spirit of God restraining us, for good reasons related to our own person, from that line of work. But our main point here is to refute the notion of guilt by mere implication through cooperative work within systems that include and profit from evil. This by itself cannot be a condition for judging our noninvolvement. The incarnation of Jesus into the social world of Roman antiquity encourages us to believe that we can, indeed, vigorously work within our own world without necessarily losing our integrity. The pattern of how this might be done will emerge more clearly when we consider the Master's public life and teachings.

The Social and Economic Identity of Jesus' Followers

When Jesus entered the public stage his keynote speech came in the synagogue at Nazareth. There he read the scroll of Isaiah 61:1-2 and stunned the congregation by applying it to himself. "The Spirit of the Lord is upon me, because he has anointed me to bring good news to the poor" (Lk 4:18). Scholars mostly agree that Jesus envisioned his mission as a cosmic jubilee and ultimate day of release for the poor.[38] Later in the Gospel when the followers of John the Baptist asked him anxiously if he was indeed the Messiah, he implied that all the signs were visible: "the blind receive their sight, the lame walk, the lepers are cleansed, the deaf hear, the dead are raised, the poor have good news brought to them" (Lk 7:22).[39]

The statements about "the poor" in these texts raise very difficult and important questions about economic life. Many theologians believe that the original "Jesus movement" arose among the poor of his society.[40] This assumption is very widespread. However, recent evidence has forced scholars to doubt whether it is true. The social origins of Christianity were much more complex than most people realize.[41] For example, Wayne Meeks traces the social origins of the first urban Christians to the merchant class of artisans and tradesmen who flourished in all the main cities. If Christianity was essentially a "proletarian" movement, hostile to the merchant classes, how then do we account for the gospel's appeal among those classes? The Pauline church did not arise among the poor or proletariat, Meeks states, "no matter how congenial it may be to Marxist historians and to those bourgeois writers who tended to romanticize poverty."[42]

Quite the contrary, Christianity spread and triumphed in the Roman Empire largely because it penetrated and transformed its social systems. It is true that some Christians did live in separation, as we have seen, but the majority did not. Meeks shows that the early congregations in the empire "generally reflected a fair cross-section of urban society."[43] In fact, he writes, "There is no specific evidence of people who are destitute—such as hired menials and dependent handworkers; the poorest of the poor, peasants, agricultural slaves, and hired agricultural day laborers, are absent."[44] According to Meeks, the "typical" Christian was "a free artisan or a small trader." Moreover, "the wealthy provided housing, meeting places, and other services for individual Christians and for whole groups. In effect, they filled the roles of patrons."[45] If Meeks is at all right, then, as some of my friends have long suspected, businesspeople were the backbone of the church, not objects of its contempt.

The Gospels themselves suggest that this pattern, decribed by Meeks among the Pauline communities, goes back to the economic identity of Jesus and his disciples. When we think of Jesus' "followers," we should think of three distinct groups.[46] First were the "disciples," who left their homes, work and families to travel with Jesus. They included the Twelve, the Seventy and quite a few others, such as Mary Magdalene. The second was a network of sympathizers who "followed" Jesus by staying where they were. The third group was the "multitudes" who flocked to Jesus everywhere he went. We need to look briefly at the social and economic identities of each group.

The twelve disciples who traveled with Jesus came from an interesting variety of social and economic backgrounds. We know most about Peter, James, John and Andrew, who were Galilean fishermen. To imagine them as "poor fisherfolk," as Sider does, is very misleading. These men were hardly poor by the standards of the time, either in social respect or in economic security. They were good Jews who were self-employed in family businesses. We cannot say exactly how prosperous they were, but, as we saw earlier, research indicates that fishing on the lake in Galilee generated some wealth and a lively commercial industry, mainly because fish was the main staple of diet there. The Gospels record that these men had their own boats, nets and even servants. Peter's mother-in-law owned a house in Capernaum that was large enough to serve as home base for Jesus and all of his disciples. And the claim that "they left everything," which all the Gospels stress as an act of sacrifice and courage, has the intended moral weight only if they left behind wealth and security enough to make it so. Otherwise, it is little more than an act of desperation. (More in the next chapter on the nature of this "disinvestment.")

The background of Levi the tax collector is somewhat more complex. His name indicates that he was Jewish, but his profession shows that he had gone to work for the Roman tax system. This would have cost him in moral and social standing among his people. From a religious point of view he was poor in these realms. He was in fact poor in a sense that was repugnant to any good Jew (not in the sense of the "righteous poor," or rich). But even if he was nothing more than the third-level manager of a toll booth, as seems likely, he was not poor in material wealth. The Gospels note that he owned a house and that leaving everything behind was a momentous event for him. It is intriguing that, before leaving, he "gave a great banquet for [Jesus] in his house; and there was a large crowd of tax collectors and others sitting at the table with them" (Lk 5:29). His context squares most closely with what I earlier labeled the class of "unrighteous rich."

The second group of people, those who "followed" Jesus from afar, were also above the economic average. We think of Peter's mother-in-law, Lazarus and his sisters, Mary and Martha, wealthy men like Joseph of Arimathea, and the wealthy women "who provided for them [Jesus and his disciples] out of their resources" (Lk 8:3). As Meeks says later Christians would do, these followers expressed their faith in Jesus by providing funds, bases of operation and moral support in their towns and communities. Again, we do not catch the stereotype of early Christian poverty in these texts. Martin Hengel has thus written that Jesus' closest followers were not poor, but mainly came from a social and economic background similar to his own.[47] This seems correct. They came mainly from the middle of the social and economic spectrum of that place and time. At the risk of shattering popular stereotypes, we might view most of them as the "righteous middle," while some were "righteous rich."

Finally, there were the multitudes who came to hear Jesus and to be healed by him. This group was obviously marked by the deepest signs of oppression. Sick, lame, blind and deaf, they came to him to be healed and to hear his words of wisdom and hope. But even here we must be careful with our economic terms. Later we shall see that the "multitudes" were not defined entirely by economic poverty. Some of the people who came to Jesus in the crowds were financially secure and even rich. The Roman centurion who begged Jesus to heal his servant was wealthy. The chief tax collector, Zacchaeus, was very rich. The woman (no doubt a former prostitute) who poured a whole bottle of nard on Jesus' hair had money enough. Indeed, all of them were people of the margins. In the social sense, they were poor, in different ways. But their marginal existence in Israel was the condition for a deeper "poverty" still, one that Jesus' followers all had in common. It was their spiritual poverty, a little different for each in every social and economic situation, that blossomed into living faith.

On the other hand, the misery of this group seems almost to have been overwhelming. And the Gospels encourage us to think of the multitudes as the very poor, to whom Jesus came especially with good news. The Gospels create no classification (as does Proverbs) for the "unrighteous poor." I am not aware of any passage in the Gospels where the very poor in wealth are also accused of being very poor in righteousness, or where these two conditions are connected. I believe it is right to say, theologically, that the poor are simply those whom Jesus blessed and to whom he proclaimed the good news. There is, I believe, a silent resistance to our tendency to blame the poor for the many things associated with their condition, and to use this as an excuse not to help them. But again, there is more to come, below, on Jesus' teachings about blessing, wealth and poverty.

In sum, neither the original circumstances of Jesus' life nor the thrust of his initial mission shows a peculiar "identification" with the economic poor, at least not of the sort that is commonly meant today. If anything, there is an unromantic and not very spectacular identification with the ordinary, the uncomplicated, the hardworking, the productive, the humble and the simply happy. But there is also a predilection for the unpredictable. The gathering of tax collectors, centurions and whores is hard to classify, for they were sometimes rich in goods but abysmally poor in social standing and in their moral lives. And there is finally that moment of truth in liberation theology, which we have seen throughout the Old Testament and now in the face of Jesus. It is the eye of the king of this universe on the innocent ones who suffer worst in his world. Their poverty does not ensure their righteousness, but his righteousness ensures that justice will be done for them.

Perhaps it is possible to think of Jesus' life and movement in this way: Jesus led relatively privileged people into new lives of economic redemption and redemptiveness. As he pulled them out of their safe worlds of social and economic stability, he placed them in contact with the beating soul of the suffering world. And the poor he called into this field of redemption. By bringing them together, the rich (in all the relevant senses) and the poor (in all senses), he created a new community that was electrified by the power of grace and liberation for everyone, in different ways. In a strange way the rich became "poor" and the poor became "rich." At bottom, this was the expression of poverty or lowering of spirit by one group in order to free and empower the spirits of the other one. And the economic expression of this was not a leveling, or egalitarianism, but something very like the order of the exodus people of Israel under the laws of Moses. The rich did not so much enter into economic poverty, for the sake of the poor, as they did into a new life of economic dynamism, power born of renewed compassion, and they went on a way that they could never have dreamed of in the quieter days before the dream of Jesus took them and made them great in the kingdom of God.

7

THE CHRIST
OF RADICAL
COMPASSION
& DELIGHT

Foxes have holes, and birds of the air have nests; but the Son of Man has nowhere to lay his head.

MATTHEW 8:20

The Son of Man came eating and drinking, and they say, "Look, a glutton and a drunkard, a friend of tax collectors and sinners!"

MATTHEW 11:19

Jesus left his family, home and work to begin his fateful public mission at about the age of thirty. Early on, he called twelve men to follow him as disciples. They ate, drank, slept, learned and worked together in a common life, until Jesus' death by crucifixion.

We have explored the basic social and economic origins of Jesus and his followers. But there is another, very important side to the question of their economic identities. Apart from their origins, we wonder what sort of economic life they *adopted* during their public mission. We wonder how they lived, and how this matters to Christians today.

Christian tradition has generally believed that Jesus and his disciples chose to live in poverty. However, there are good reasons to doubt this time-honored tradition. In this chapter we shall see that it creates very serious problems in interpreting the Gospels.[1] Not least is the difficulty raised by New Testament scholar Luke Johnson. He observes (contrary to common opinion) that the Gospels seem to give conflicting messages about Christian economic life.[2]

Indeed, sometimes it seems that Jesus is two different persons. The "radical Jesus" left everything for the sake of the kingdom of God. For this Jesus life is heavy-laden, sorrowful and without place. He is the Son of Man who has "nowhere to lay his head." He lacks all sentiment for earthly ties of any kind, and he urgently commands people to abandon their families, possessions and jobs—and even their lives—to follow him. This Jesus cloaks all of life in a dark shroud of severity, and he grinds on ceaselessly toward death on the cross.

On the other side, however, is a Jesus whom Christian tradition has largely ignored. He is the celebrative King, the Son of Man who "came eating and drinking" with his lost people, whom he now has found. He lacks all moderation or pious restraint. He celebrates life with such intensity that it was shocking to the religious community. To their stiff souls, his life was like a wild, embarrassing dance, breaking all decorum. And they did not think of him as an irrepressibly joyous King David, flush with the glow of victory. In the grapevines of gossip he was known rather as the wanton son of Deuteronomy, "a glutton and a drunkard," whom the people should put to death. But his disciples and the multitudes saw this Jesus differently; to be with him was to be bathed in warm light. To them, he was not severe or oppressive. On the contrary, he lifted their many burdens. His very presence brought peace, good cheer and a mood of joyous celebration that could not be contained by the old wineskins. His essence was not severity and death but lightness and life. And those who followed him were not impoverished. Rather, they found powerful new expressions of delight and compassion in their economic lives. To them he brought new power. For them, Jesus was indeed the Christ of compassion and delight.

I believe that both of these images of Jesus must go into our portrait of his economic life.[3] Somehow (in order to understand Christian economic life itself) we must better comprehend the life of Jesus in both its moments of suffering and delight, severity and lightness, sacrifice and flourishing. Our tradition has not always done this. But we will see that material poverty is not a good description of his chosen life. Nor does it well describe the lives that he enjoined on his followers. Indeed, it is difficult to identify the principles that guided him, and (more urgently) that ought to guide us. That is the burden of this present chapter.

The Life and Demands of "the Radical Jesus"

First let us consider the texts that seem to present the life and demands of Jesus as a radical negation of wealth, and as a universal call to poverty. All of the Gospels (but especially Luke's) stress the radical call of Jesus to surrender possessions and to lead lives of sacrificial suffering. Luke writes that the four fishermen, Peter, James, John and Andrew, and also the tax collector, Levi, "left *everything,* and followed him" (Lk 5:28; see Mk 2:13-17; Mt 9:9-13). When volunteers came running, Jesus pushed them away like overenthusiastic pups. "Foxes have holes, and birds of the air have nests," he would say to one of them, "but the Son of Man has nowhere to lay his head" (Lk 9:57-58).

The encounter with the rich young ruler (Lk 18:18-29; Mt 19:16-22; Mk 10:17-22) is a prime example of Jesus' severity. The man was a paragon of virtue, an original "success story." He was a "ruler," quite possibly a member of the prestigious Sanhedrin, and "was very rich."

He seemed a perfect model of what we called the "righteous rich," a man both godly and blessed with wealth. We are unsure of his motives, but he approached Jesus with this apparently sincere question: "Good Teacher, what must I do to inherit eternal life?"

If the man expected pious small talk and a polite "Good day!" from this young rabbi, he got the surprise of his life. He soon found himself in a tangle of theological barbed wire. Jesus' sharp response must have seemed uncalled for. "Why do you call me good? No one is good but God alone." After a presumably tense moment of silence, he answered the man's question: "You know the commandments," and he tersely went through the all-too-familiar checklist. With no idea that he was about to hang himself, the rich man answered back, "I have kept all these since my youth." The poor man had failed to notice the obvious. Jesus had omitted the commandment "Thou shalt not covet."

Jesus tightened the wire. "There is still one thing lacking. Sell all that you own and distribute the money to the poor, and you will have treasure in heaven; then come, follow me." The Gospels all record that the man was overcome by sorrow when he heard these words, "for," as Matthew writes, "he had many possessions" (Mt 19:22). Perhaps he looked back over his shoulder into the eyes of Jesus, who called out: "How hard it is for those who have wealth to enter the kingdom of God! Indeed, it is easier for a camel to go through the eye of a needle than for someone who is rich to enter the kingdom of God" (Lk 18:24-25).

We must understand that Jesus did not present this to the rich man as an option—it was a requirement. The astonishing thing is that he made it a requirement for the man's salvation! To inherit eternal life, he must get rid of his possessions and leave the tangle of his economic life behind. Otherwise, he was doomed.[4]

This severity seems to defy all known biblical wisdom. Jesus implies that the man cannot be righteous before God and rich in possessions at the same time. Indeed, it seems that Jesus extends this rule to all rich people. Only with God, he says, is it possible that a "rich man" be spared eternal death. Rather than liberating the poor from poverty, in an odd reversal of Old Testament thought, Jesus seems to call the rich to be saved *through* poverty.

The encounter between Jesus and the rich young ruler culminates a theme that Luke has developed purposefully from the beginning of his narrative. The command to abandon everything has expanded to become a terribly intimidating formula for repentance and salvation. A bitter argument between brothers over an inheritance prompted the now-famous words of Jesus to the disciples: "Therefore I tell you, do not worry about your life, what you will eat, or about your body, what you will wear. For life is more than food, and the body more than clothing" (Lk 12:22-23). Instead, he advised them to consider the ravens, which "neither sow nor reap," and the lilies, which "neither toil nor spin." He continued: "And do not keep striving for what you are to eat and what you are to drink, and do not keep worrying. For *it is the nations of the world that strive after all these things.*" They should instead seek the kingdom. Then came the radical command: "Sell your possessions, and give alms. Make purses for yourselves that do not wear out, an unfailing treasure in heaven, where no thief comes near and no moth destroys. For where your treasure is, there your heart will be also" (Lk 12:33-34; italics mine).

When Jesus sent his disciples in pairs "to proclaim the kingdom of God and to heal" (Lk 9:2), he ordered them to take "no staff, nor bag, nor bread, nor money—not even an extra tunic" (Lk 9:3). Later, he sent the Seventy with similar orders: "Carry no purse, no bag, no sandals; and greet no one on the road" (Lk 10:4). In another place he made the request to anyone who would follow him: "So therefore, none of you can become my disciple if you do not give up all your possessions" (Lk 14:33).

In Luke's version of the Beatitudes, the "radical Jesus" reaches his

highest standard of severity. He spoke to his disciples:
> Blessed are you who are poor,[5]
>> for yours is the kingdom of God.
> Blessed are you who are hungry now,
>> for you will be filled.
> Blessed are you who weep now,
>> for you will laugh. (Lk 6:20-21)

And in contrast, he pronounced these awful woes on the rich:
> But woe to you who are rich,
>> for you have received your consolation.
> Woe to you who are full now,
>> for you will be hungry.
> Woe to you who are laughing now,
>> for you will mourn and weep.
> Woe to you when all speak well of you, for that is what their ancestors did to the false prophets. (Lk 6:24-27)

Thus spoke the radical Jesus.

How are we to interpret and apply these texts? The most obvious, literal interpretation is that Jesus believed that having and enjoying possessions was the spiritual death of human beings. To him, then, simply having possessions, much less enjoying them in abundance or excess, testified to our lack of real faith in *God*. However, historic Christianity (even monasticism) has wisely understood that this interpretation cannot be true.[6] The main reason is that it characterizes the material world and its extensions as a realm that is poisonous and evil, comparable, say, to a radioactive landscape. This interpretation thus defines our position in that realm (the created order) as an evil state of being.[7] So if this creation is not good, but evil, then (as the Gnostics openly admitted) the Creator was not good in bringing it about. Our whole idea of "the good" *in* the physical realm turns out instead to be a grotesquely perverse model for basic evil. We had thought that providing our children with shelter, pleasant surroundings (a nice toy or two) and a stable income were *good* things. But we have actually placed them in a deadly situation and have committed the unwitting murder of our own loved ones. Worse, we have done this monstrous thing at God's instigation. In such actions, God performs evil, and so do we. (Hence Gnostics viewed the Creator as an evil spirit.) And if our material culture is actually the realm of God's displeasure, then the biblical mandate to empower the poor by using the mechanisms of that culture (job training, home buying, investment strategies and so on) can hardly be called "liberation." Scripture rather designs a menu for making the poor displeasing to God.

But if Jesus did not believe that the material world was essentially a realm of evil, how are we to interpret his life of poverty and its demands? None of the traditional explanations seem quite satisfactory. As noted, Catholic theology teaches that Jesus' poverty is an ideal for a blessed few rather than a rule of faith and life for everyone. Jesus' blessing of poverty was not also a cursing of wealth, but the establishing of a higher plane of good and a lower one. One difficulty here, though, is that our texts make the stronger claim that Jesus' radical demands are valid for *anyone* who would be a Christian. If these demands require poverty, then they require it of *all* Christians. On the other hand, mainline Protestants typically limit Jesus' poverty to the unique circumstances of his mission to suffer and die. That he was poor established neither the cursing of wealth nor the higher ideal of poverty. Rather, his poverty was essential to his unique mission. His life of suffering is not for us to imitate, but to venerate, and more loosely to emulate. But this explanation also seems to evade the strong connections in the Gospels, especially Luke's, between Jesus' own economic life and the obligations of all his disciples likewise to follow.

Recent versions of liberation theology understand this and have rightly insisted that all Christians must face the "radical Jesus" more directly. But their attempt to make the poverty of Jesus a model for the social and political liberation of the poor seems both strained and confusing. It seems strained because the Gospels do not obviously picture Jesus' life as a means of liberating the poor. On the contrary, it seems that he blessed the poor *because* of their poverty.[8] It also seems confusing to say that Jesus blessed poverty, but that this blessing is a vision for enriching the poor.

Our tradition that Jesus and his disciples adopted "blessed" lives of poverty thus creates serious problems. Before proposing a way of resolving the problem, though, I believe it is time that we seriously consider a second image of Jesus that our tradition and contemporary moral theology have largely passed over. The Gospels also present Jesus as the Christ of compassion and delight. If we face this image of the Lord, I believe we will conclude that he did not live in material poverty and that we must reconsider our understanding of his demands and our obligations in economic life.

Facing the Christ of Compassion and Delight

This second image of Jesus shows powerfully that he did not demolish the Old Testament vision, as the Scribes and Pharisees, and later the Gnostics, accused him of doing. On the contrary, his life was a new incarnation of royal effect. In him (to use geometric terms) all the complex lines of "the law and the prophets" came together into a single point. It is true that, for a little while, the boldest lines of the vision—dominion and delight—became very difficult to make out in the concentrated point of the Christ-event and its intense lowliness and darkness. But from behind the dark cloud that blotted out the sun of God's power and goodness, the old vision appeared again in new form, its several lines fanning out to open the world of dominion and delight to Christians, now tested and true. And the hardest texts (to which we shall return) do not, after all, contradict this claim. They help us to see and to comprehend its deep, mysterious truth. With the "surgeon's bleeding hands," to use Eliot's phrase, the "radical Jesus" re-created our dignity and empowered us, as new creatures, to begin again as servant-lords.

A Drunkard and a Glutton

In responding to the authorities who had arrested John the Baptist, Jesus revealed a side of his character that Christians, especially those from traditions of pietism and modern liberalism, have not appreciated enough. That is the joy and celebrativeness of his character. With obvious contempt he accused the authorities ("those who put on fine clothing") of jailing John because of his greatness. At risk to his own safety, Jesus spoke publicly in John's defense, declaring him "more than a prophet"; "among those born of women no one is greater" (Lk 7:24-26). By silencing John, he alleged, those in power exposed themselves as mere "children sitting in the marketplace and calling to one another: 'We played the flute for you, and you did not dance; we wailed, and you did not weep' " (Lk 7:32). They could not domesticate this wild man, for he would not play by their childish rules. So they demonized him and used their superior power to crush him. John came "eating no bread and drinking no wine, and you say, 'He has a demon' " (Lk 7:33).

But if they could not contain John's wild, uncompromising asceticism, they were certainly too small-spirited to cope with Jesus. For his life of joyous celebration went to an extreme that to them was even more dangerous. It led down the steep slope to revelry, wantonness and sin. Unlike John, the "Son of Man has come eating and drinking, and you say, 'Look, a glutton and a drunkard, a friend of tax collectors and "sinners." ' " (Lk 7:34). In Deuteronomy they found the "right" Scripture for Jesus. He was the wanton, disobedient son with no regard for his parents, who should be put to death. Of their son the parents should say, "He is a glutton and a drunkard" (Deut 21:20). Jesus came cavorting, a drunkard and glutton among "tax collectors and sinners." They would not see in this man's life the true "Son of

Man," the dancing King of Israel, celebrating his presence with the lost people of the earth. But that is who, and what, Jesus was.

Scholar Richard Horsely, who is known for his stress on the radical social side of Jesus' mission, nonetheless makes this very important comment on the Gospels' portrait of Jesus and his disciples:

> A strikingly distinctive activity of Jesus and his followers was their regular celebration with festive meals, almost certainly a celebration of the presence of the kingdom. . . . A surprising amount of the gospel tradition has to do with feeding, table fellowship, and related teachings . . . leading to the conclusion that Jesus and his followers were indeed celebrating the presence of the kingdom.[9]

Horsely stresses that "Jesus had a reputation for 'eating and drinking,' one which led opponents to accuse him of associating with people who were indulgently enjoying life rather than observing the Torah."[10] In contrast to our tradition, it seems that Jesus and his followers lived a celebrative life, which expressed the reality of the kingdom of God in the *present*. Apparently the lifestyle was exuberant enough to make the religious authorities wonder (on the occasion of a "great banquet" given at Levi's house) why Jesus and his disciples did not observe the tradition of fasting, but instead were eating and drinking. He responded by asking, "You cannot make wedding guests fast while the bridegroom is with them, can you?" (Lk 5:29-34). Jesus compared his appearance to "new wine" that simply bursts the old wineskins of Jewish piety (Lk 5:36-39).

This answer puts the whole tradition of Jesus' "poverty" into the class of "old wineskins" that cannot well contain the powerful new wine that was Jesus. For as Horsely writes, "God was [in Christ] finally feeding the people with miraculous abundance despite appearances of paucity."[11] Indeed, Jesus called his disciples to *leave* but not exactly to become *poor* in material things. There was indeed a moment of "poverty" about their new existence, and we must say more about this, but they did not live in want of good things. As Pilgrim states, "Luke's portrayal of Jesus' life depicts a person who rejoices in life and accepts the goodness of God's creation, including some of the things that only money can buy."[12]

Several episodes in Jesus' life reveal him as the Christ of delight. At the wedding feast at Cana, when the hosts ran out of wine (Jn 2:1-11), Jesus rescued them from humiliation (at his mother's insistence) by turning the six purification vats of water into about 180 gallons of the very best wine. He thus performed this very first of his miracles, which "revealed his glory" as the true King (Jn 2:11), simply to preserve a precious moment of celebration and delight for his friends. Another episode involved the woman who poured precious nard on Jesus (Mk 14:3; Jn 12:3). She was probably disreputable. And the event seemed so wasteful, so thoroughly wanton and improper, that it drove one of his disciples to the enemy. This earnest disciple unleashed a moral tirade on his Master for allowing luxurious perfume (worth about a year's income to a day laborer) to be wasted on himself. It could have been sold to help the poor. That disciple (whose reasoning sounds decidedly familiar) was of course Judas. Like the Pharisees, his joyless moralism betrayed and destroyed him.

Other texts indicate clearly that Jesus did not (in spite of traditions that seem to claim the contrary) demand that all his followers leave their homes, much less that they become poor. We think again of the many "bit players" who made no headlines in the biblical story. They were there, working behind the scenes in their own unspectacular ways. They, too, "followed" Jesus, but not by leaving their work, families and jobs behind. Their economic lives expressed Christian faith in other ways. We think again of Mary, Martha and Lazarus, who had a house in Bethany, near Jerusalem, which they opened freely to Jesus during his travels. We think of Peter's mother-in-law, who owned a large house with servants. She gave all this to Jesus by making it a vital base of operation in Galilee. We also remember the several women who "provided for them out of their resources" (Lk

8:3). Jesus depended on these women for financial backing and support. By putting their money to this use (rather than, say, simply giving it away to the poor) they, too, became his disciples. This relationship suggests that neither Jesus nor his followers operated without regard for where their next meal would come from. Even the inner circle of disciples left their possessions without abandoning them. After Jesus' death, we learn that Peter had kept his "capital" in storage. He brought his boat and nets out of the dust and went back to his business of fishing. All of these examples strongly support Luke Johnson's judgment:

> The poverty of Jesus is not to be found first in his lack of material possessions, for he and his followers seemed to have received support from others (Luke 8:1-3) and had sufficient funds to help the poor (John 13:29). The poverty of Jesus is to be found first in his faith. It is, properly speaking, a theological poverty.[13]

Our encounter with the chief tax collector Zacchaeus will deepen our comprehension of this kind of "poverty."

Zacchaeus: From Oppressor to Servant-Lord

The story of Zacchaeus (recorded only in Luke) helps to lay out a creative pattern for the right use of wealth by Christians. Nearing the end of his Gospel, Luke records this story about a chief tax collector who had sold his birthright for the pottage of Rome's gold. Later we shall understand how this story, which Luke connected with certain parables given by Jesus, carries with it a kind of resolution of tensions that have mounted in the narrative. Through moral prostitution Zacchaeus had become rich at the expense of the poor. To pious Jews, he personified demonic structural evil. No righteous person would have anything to do with him. It must have been unbelievable to the disciples that Jesus, who had sent people like the respected rich young ruler away in humiliation and sorrow, now received a man of Zacchaeus's character without even a word of rebuke or warning about severe moral requirements. In the context of Luke's thematic development, the two encounters face each other, begging for resolution of the tension between them.[14] The inconsistency was not lost on the crowds, who muttered that he had "gone to be the guest of one who is a sinner" (Lk 19:7).[15]

The astonishing thing about this final encounter is that it breaks the moral pattern in Luke where we least expect it. In contrast to the other meetings (with people a good deal more righteous than Zacchaeus), Jesus utters not a word of demand. There is nothing about selling everything and leaving. There is an amazing silence on the matter of Zacchaeus's job within that economic system. Jesus simply goes home with him.

Zacchaeus himself determined the requirements for his new life. He constructed his plan from the laws of the Old Testament. In cases of theft, the law required that the guilty person pay the victim *twice* the amount stolen. In very bad cases, the amount could be greater (Ex 22:8-9; 2 Sam 12:6). As a token of his sincerity Zacchaeus promised Jesus that he would give *half* of his possessions to the poor. He also promised to make an inquiry into the fraud that might have occurred under his watch: "If I have defrauded anyone of anything, I will pay back four times as much" (Lk 19:8). Hearing this, Jesus simply declared, "Today salvation has come to this house, because he too is a son of Abraham. For the Son of Man came to seek out and to save the lost" (Lk 19:9-10).

The established pattern of the story makes it striking that Zacchaeus (of all people) did not give away *all* of his possessions. He gave half. Then, all on his own (rather than following some radical new ethic), he rigorously applied the Old Testament codes of justice to himself. The whole movement of the story changes the expected direction. Zacchaeus does not leave his house, under requirements from Jesus, to follow him and thereby find his salvation. Instead, Jesus goes to Zacchaeus, who announces and authorizes his own requirements, and salvation comes "today" to *him!*

In this story something is recovered that had seemed lost in the severity of Jesus' demands. Zacchaeus takes us back into a renewed form of the Old Testament vision. We begin to glimpse again the possible goodness of working *in* the world and *using* wealth for righteousness. We also begin to glimpse again the idea of true dominion wherein God gives people freedom (within limits) to establish their own economic lives. A light of redemption begins to glimmer from within even this very corrupt economic system. Its source is Zacchaeus's personal transformation. This former lord of oppression becomes, amazingly, a powerful agent of redemption for vulnerable people. In his transformation, the system itself becomes an unlikely instrument of power in the kingdom of God.

I do not wish to say that Christians can work through *any* economic system, for it is certainly possible (as the example of Sodom and Gomorrah shows) for systems to become irredeemably evil. Hitler's Germany and the systems of global communism may illustrate this qualification. But, like the incarnate economic identity of Jesus, the case of Zacchaeus ought to be a great encouragement to Christian people who do not believe themselves to be called away from their professional work. This seems to me a story of "world-openness," what Wolterstorff has called "world-formative" Christianity,[16] rather than one of withdrawal or fear of the world. His story encourages us to find ways of unleashing the light of transformation and true dominion. Like Zacchaeus, we can find creative ways to shape our institutions—families, churches, schools, banks, corporations, businesses and also our larger political system—into instruments of redemptive power. At least we can seek to become agents of such power within them.

But to the second point about his freedom. Zacchaeus made his own yoke. Part of it he built from the Old Testament law; the other part came apparently from his own moral sense. It seemed right to him to give away half of his possessions. He offers this to Jesus. Now Jesus might have said, "Half, Zacchaeus? That is a good beginning. But you must sell *everything*, give the proceeds to the poor, and then follow me." But he did not say this. In Jesus' acceptance of Zacchaeus's vision of a redeemed and redemptive economic life, Zacchaeus regains his freedom and dignity. Jesus recovers Zacchaeus's dignity from the indignant moralism of the crowds, who would not have accepted ten pounds of flesh as satisfaction. The matter is essentially between Zacchaeus and the Lord, who, in a stunning moment, pronounces with authority, "because he too is a son of Abraham."

What was it that made Zacchaeus's actions acceptable to Jesus? One thing stands clear. Unlike the rich young ruler, who would not face his need even after it had been made public, Zacchaeus had come to the end of himself and was desperate to come clean and turn his life around. Such people seem to have been pulled by some irresistible power toward Jesus. The lost sheep knew the voice of their shepherd. Jesus needed no barbed wire to bring Zacchaeus to the fold. He may have been a disgusting man (I picture Louie DePalma, the corrupt little runt, played by Danny De Vito, who ran the cab company in the TV series "Taxi"), but somehow, through the night of his guilt, his heart had become good. Zacchaeus was rich in wealth, but he knew that he was poor in what mattered most. The most essential thing, I believe, is the poverty of spirit that infused all of his words and actions with righteousness and made them acceptable to the Lord.

Yet his virtue was not only in spirit. Although Zacchaeus did not give away everything, his actions made a dramatic testimony in the visible economic world to the reality of the change in his heart. Zacchaeus had an obvious desire to bring about real justice. His actions were not symbolic gestures of charity, like giving fruit baskets to the poor at Christmas. Rather like old Scrooge in Dickens's *A Christmas Carol*, he meant really to do something for the poor. We can only imagine the effect of his transformation on the people who lived within his "realm." The house of Zacchaeus that had once, like Tolkien's Dark Tower, cast its shadow of oppression on everything for miles around, now became a place of light, merriment, mercy, justice and relief for people. From this powerful position he could infect the whole environment with his passion for goodness and truth.

Furthermore, presuming that he stayed at his job, there is no reason to think that his sacrifices made him even marginally poor. It seems obvious that his income would eventually overtake the cost of his reparations. However, he went somewhat beyond the strict requirements of the law in paying back fourfold and giving half of his goods to the poor. We do not know if he moved into a smaller house, or at exactly to what level his new lifestyle settled. But more important than the statistical margin or "dollar figure" of his economic comedown was the spirit that infused his actions with righteousness. In these actions, Jesus sensed what Amos missed in the unrighteous rich of Israel. He sensed the grieving that breeds compassion, love and redemptive action toward the poor. I know of no fixed sum or rule that can reliably measure true grieving in the heart. In this case it was not completely a private matter, for he acted within the traditions of Israel, but it was almost that. As the disapproving crowds looked on, Zacchaeus somehow knew what to do, and Jesus knew a son of Abraham when he saw one. This blessing without question counts this rich man among the "poor" whom Jesus called "blessed."

Facing the "Radical Jesus" Again

The "Christ of delight" teaches us that proper grieving comes through sorrow to celebration. Jesus and his followers lived a life of freedom and lightness, even as the Master moved relentlessly toward Jerusalem to suffer and die. Both the inner and outer circles of disciples made sacrifices, but in return all received a place at Jesus' royal table. However, we must still offer a convincing interpretation of the "radical

Jesus" in the hard texts above, to show that he and the "Christ of delight" are not two persons, but one and the same Lord.

Another look at the sending of the Twelve and the Seventy will help to confirm this claim. We must understand this powerful scene in its context. At this point in the story something earthshaking is about to occur. Until now, Jesus has revealed himself as someone with extraordinary powers. With a word he commands demons, forgives sins, heals diseases and raises the dead. He has authority over every existing realm. Even the winds and the seas obey him, just as they obeyed the Lord God when he created the earth, destroyed and recreated it in Noah's time, and when he redeemed Israel through the raging seas of the exodus. Through Jesus the power and dominion of *the Lord* is present on earth.

As scholar Heinz Schürmann writes, "Clearly with the sending of the Twelve, something new is beginning."[17] For the first time, the power of Jesus began to overflow to his disciples. "Then Jesus called the twelve together and gave them power and authority over all demons and to cure diseases" (Lk 9:1). The passages that follow suggest that the first mission was imperfect, for the disciples fret over food, are powerless to cast out a certain demon and bicker among themselves about greatness. But after the second mission (Lk 10:1-23), the Seventy "returned with joy, saying, 'Lord, in your name even the demons submit to us'" (Lk 10:17). Even the demons! At this Jesus is so overcome with joy that he bursts forth in exclamation and prayerful thanksgiving to his Father. At last, he has seen his ancient enemy, Satan, "fall from heaven like a flash of lightning" (Lk 10:18, 21). These "infants" have felled him. This event marks the beginning of what all the prophets and kings of Israel longed to see, but did not (Lk 10:24). The kingdom of God had taken root on earth.

What does all this have to do with economic life and interpreting the radical Jesus? We must understand that this was the critical moment to which he had called them. It was the moment of truth when he revealed that he was more than a mere rabbi or prophet. He was the Christ, the Messiah of God, the King of Israel and of all the earth. It was also the moment when he revealed *their* share in his power and dominion. It was time to give them power such as the world had not yet seen, nor would see again. By the Spirit of God the strongholds of darkness would be broken and God's rule would be established forever on the earth.

We must try to imagine what this would have been like for them. They were at his right hand when he fed thousands in the wilderness (Lk 9:10-17). After this, when he asked them, "Who do the crowds say that I am?" (Lk 9:18), Peter answered correctly, "The Messiah of God" (Lk 9:20). The secret was out, the words were true, but their effect was deadly. The disciples understood "the Messiah" as a term of raw power and dominion, and now as the means by which *they* would attain it. As their imaginations swelled, Jesus sternly explained that "The Son of Man must undergo great suffering, and be rejected . . . and be killed" (Lk 9:22). This is the context for some of his most sorrowful and severe actions and words. It was then that he said to them, "If any want to become my followers, let them deny themselves and take up their cross daily and follow me" (Lk 9:23). It was as they pondered world power at Jesus' right hand that he spoke the terrible words: "For those who want to save their life will lose it, and those who lose their life for my sake will save it. What does it profit them if they gain the whole world, but lose or forfeit themselves?" (Lk 9:24-25).

Peter, John and James stood with him on the mountaintop when he was "transfigured" and met with Moses and Elijah (Lk 9:28-36). On the next day we find them powerless to cast out a demon, and Jesus rebukes them sharply for being faithless and perverse (Lk 9:37-43). And as they marveled at his power over the demon, he repeated his words about his destiny to suffer and die, but "they did not understand" (Lk 9:44-45). Next, "an argument arose among them as to which of them was the greatest" (Lk 9:46). At this Jesus lifted up a child and said to them, "Whoever welcomes this child in my name welcomes me, and whoever welcomes me welcomes the one who sent me; for the least among all of you is the greatest" (Lk 9:48). The stunning implication is that power will come only if their arrogance is cast out by the childlike disposition of God.

This was the context for Jesus' words about his own path of suffering. He had "set his face to go to Jerusalem" to die (Lk 9:51-56) when a man unwittingly offered to go with him. Jesus' life of celebration and power, which the disciples thought had only just begun, was at its end. The victorious empowerment of his disciples was, ironically, the signal that his hour had come. The kingdom was established in them, but he was now uprooted from the earth, with "nowhere to lay his head." It was time to go to the cross.

The "radical command" to the Twelve, the Seventy and the others (such as the rich young ruler) was not a negation of wealth or even a requirement to live their entire lives without possessions. It was rather that negative moment of truth when they must be prepared as no human beings before or after them to initiate the kingdom of Jesus Christ on earth. It is a lesson that the "righteous rich" find hardest of all to learn. (Zacchaeus, being well aware of his unrighteousness, had no difficulty with it.) Being "first," they must therefore become "last."

To be at the right and left hand of the king was blessed, indeed, but it was not to be envied. Jesus placed them on a thin, dizzyingly high spiritual peak with treacherous slopes on two sides. A misstep either way could mean swift spiritual death. The one slope was the swelling sense of self-importance—the spirit that animates the fallen world. This would disarm them and the demons would not depart. The phase of radical living was for them rather like the years in the wilderness for Israel. It was not an end, but a means toward one. It was to impress on them their complete dependence on the power of

God. If they lost that sense of dependence, they were like the man who gained the world but lost his soul. They would have nothing. But on the other side of the peak was the slope of fear. Their idea of victory was all wrong, so that they were vulnerable to defeat. When Jesus, the powerful "Messiah of God," would be manhandled, humiliated, disgraced beyond words and, finally, crucified in public view, they would lose faith. The phase of radical dependency would also steel and temper them for the worst. At least it would shape the core of their memories for the difficult years to come. Even with that his crucifixion would all but shatter them.

Thus, Jesus had somehow to perform the fragile art of creating within them profound meekness and extraordinary bravery at the same time. They must have both the fearless pride of the warrior *and* the simple humility of the child. They must be great lords, but, in being that, they must be servants, least of all. This, I believe, explains the moment of physical deprivation in the larger course of their lives. It provided the right conditions of dependence on God and separation from the cares and confusion of the world that was needed in order to instill both confidence and humility in them for the time when "all these things" would be restored to them. In a context of complete dependence on God (through Jesus), removed from their normal support systems, they would learn the true identity of Christ, they would learn of their own chosen places on his right and left hand, they would partake of power the like of which the world had never seen, they would become heirs of the earth—but they would not lose their souls. The life they adopted with Jesus was not "supererogatory" or one that had its end in "virtuous poverty," but rather was a life that aimed eventually at dominion and rule with the Lord.

Jesus' words in the Upper Room on the night of his death (where the disciples again argued about who was greatest among them; Lk 22:24-28) add support to this last claim. First, he promised them unimagined dominion and delight in the future. "You are those who have stood by me in my trials; and I confer on you, just as my Father conferred on me, a kingdom, so that you may eat and drink at my table in my kingdom, and you will sit on thrones judging the twelve tribes of Israel" (Lk 22:28-30). To this he added words for the present: " 'When I sent you out without a purse, bag or sandals, did you lack anything?' They said, 'No, not a thing.' He said to them, 'But *now*, the one who has a purse must take it, and likewise a bag. And the one who has no sword must sell his cloak and buy one' " (Lk 22:35-36).[18]

Before, they went with almost nothing. They had learned what they needed to learn. But now they must arm themselves with the weapons of wealth and warfare; they must conscript human culture into the battle for the kingdom.[19]

This same double movement occurs in nearly all of the radical texts. The story of the rich young ruler comes to this enigmatic end:

Then Peter said, "Look, we have left our homes and followed you." And [Jesus] said to them, "Truly I tell you, there is no one who has left house or wife or brothers or parents or children, for the sake of the kingdom of God, who will not get back very much more in this age, and in the age to come eternal life." (Lk 18:28-30)

Perhaps no passage in the Gospels better illustrates the strange harmony between sacrifice and flourishing, weakness and power. The radical call was to both, in different ways. The lesson of the flowers and ravens shows that the disciples' dignity and delight will be returned through faith. "Instead, strive for his kingdom," Jesus says to them, "and these things [possessions] will be given to you as well" (Lk 12:31). This was not a simple formula for "health and wealth" without suffering, but neither was it a theology of servanthood without lordship. Their suffering was temporary, a "path" that existed for a purpose, which was unrepeatable. Part of that purpose was that *we* and others might later flourish and have life. You might think of the disciples as having participated in the suffering and death of Jesus, for the world, in a way that expressed their unique proximity to him.

Being closest, they suffered most, but their reward was greatest—in *this* life and in the life to come, as it was promised.

In sum, Jesus called his followers to lives of redemptive sacrifice and celebrative delight. Perhaps the outer ring of followers, including especially Zacchaeus, is the best "type" for professional people in America. These disciples call us to a renewed, perhaps more radical, form of the Old Testament vision of the righteous rich. They represented God in the world by using their power intensely as God used his in Christ. He brought out their great potential for good. They committed their possessions and their positions in the world to the work of redemption in the fullest sense of that term. A poverty of spirit animated their delight, and this proved itself in free and effective actions of good will toward the poor and the powerless. I will develop all of these points when we consider the teachings of Jesus.

8

FOUR PARABLES
ABOUT THE
RICH & THEIR
RICHES

Without a parable he told them nothing.
MATTHEW 13:34

*M*uch of Jesus' teaching is about rich people and their riches. His teaching tends to portray the rich in a negative light. The rich men in his stories are often in desperate shape, although they do not know it. For all their prudence and success, they can be shortsighted fools. For all their happiness on earth, they may be on course for torment in the life to come. As with his life, Jesus' teachings often give the impression that to be rich is to be separated from the greatest good of all—the goodness of God—and to be condemned to the worst of evils, life without God forever.

The negative accent of Jesus' teaching on wealth has provoked sweeping judgments, such as this one from Jacques Ellul:

It is the very essence of the whole life of the rich, which is *necessarily* opposed to God. Apart from the exceptional cases . . . Abraham, Job and Solomon—there is no righteous rich man, there is no

good rich man. . . . Judgment against the rich is always radical.[1]
However, Ellul's statement has caught only the radical, negative accent of Jesus' word to the rich. As we shall see, the Christ of compassion, dominion and delight was also a teacher. In his words to the rich
there was also hope, liberation and even praise. When all of our
sifting is done, his message to the rich is essentially the same as that
of Moses, the prophets and Wisdom. Most audible in these ancient
writings perhaps is the thunder of warning that rumbles to awaken
a land that has sunk into oblivion. However, the essence of prophetic
warning is not hate, but love. Its object is not to destroy the rich, but
to save them, and to shape them into the great power for good that
God has ordained and blessed them to be. I believe that this, too, was
the object of Jesus' economic life and the point of his sometimes
severe message to the rich.

This chapter is devoted to four parables that Jesus told about rich
people. We shall explore the parables of the rich fool (Lk 12:13-21),
the dishonest manager (Lk 16:1-9), the rich man and Lazarus (Lk
16:19-31) and the ten pounds (Lk 19:11-27). The first three occur only
in Luke, which again indicates his special interest in rich Christians.
All four parables come at very critical places in the Gospel, as Luke
seeks to resolve the conflicts over the economic problem, and they
thus play key roles in an unfolding plot where rich people are at last
redeemed as good and faithful servants of the king.

The Rich Fool

The parable of the rich fool dominates the landscape of Luke's important twelfth chapter. For a parable it is unusually long, and the
detailed explanation of its symbolism suggests its importance to Jesus.
It was the occasion for his discourse on the "lilies" and the "ravens,"
and it sets the stage in Luke's Gospel for a series of lessons by Jesus
on riches.

As I have noted before, the context of this chapter was a dispute between brothers over their inheritance. This bitter argument prompted Jesus to issue the warning: "Take care! Be on your guard against all kinds of *greed;* for one's life does not consist in the abundance of possessions" (Lk 12:15, italics mine). Jesus then told this story.

There was a "rich man" whose land "produced abundantly." The man thought to himself, "What shall I do, for I have no place to store my crops?" His solution was practical. He pulled down his old barns and built bigger ones. Now with his grain stored and his finances secure, the man did what you or I might do—he retired and sat back to enjoy life. But Jesus went on. The man said to himself, "You have ample goods laid up for many years; relax, eat, drink, be merry." But that very night God said to him, " 'You fool! This very night your life is being demanded of you. And the things you have prepared, whose will they be?' So it is with those who store up treasures for themselves but are not rich toward God" (Lk 12:13-21).

What are we to make of the parable? Obviously, it is a warning against "greed." But deeper questions linger. What was so greedy about the man's behavior? What was so very wrong with his life that God judged it a tale told by a "fool"? Are we any different?

Like much that Jesus said and did as a teacher, this parable upsets the balance of his disciples' moral universe. A man who appears to act wisely by the established canons of wisdom is instead denounced as a fool. Thus Jesus' teaching, and their learning, began. The rich man was hard-working and successful at farming. His harvest simply burst the seams of his old barns. He was also frugal—he had saved enough to build the newer and larger grain barns. And he was shrewd—he turned a crisis into the opportunity of a lifetime. By investing in the new barns, his return was total financial security for the rest of his life.

So what was wrong? Ronald Sider writes that the man had an "obsession with material things," as evidenced by his "greedy compulsion to acquire more and more possessions, even though he does not need them."[2] He concludes:

We cannot read the parable of the rich fool without thinking of our own society. We madly multiply more sophisticated gadgets, larger and taller buildings and faster means of transportation—not because such things truly enrich our lives but because we are driven by an obsession for more and more.[3]

But the man in the parable is not an obsessive spendthrift. He is more comparable to ordinary men and women who (we think) prudently invest in pension plans. His new barns are really no different from an IRA account, Social Security or some other tax-deferred annuity. Investments like this do immense good. They create financial security for people in old age, and they free us to enjoy some of the pleasures of life in our "sunset years." Does Jesus mean to condemn savings and retirement as covetous and worthy of damnation?

The story of the rich fool itself (in its context) suggests that it was not the creation of financial security nor the retirement and its pleasures that Jesus judged as greedy foolishness. The man's foolishness was rather in his philosophy of life, the whole disposition behind otherwise prudent actions. We must recall that Jesus aimed the parable primarily at the covetousness of the two brothers. They are thus our point of entry into its primary meaning.[4]

The brothers had lost their father. In healthy people the effects of death hang over them and their world like a woolen shroud. The bereaved continue to grieve—pondering the finality of death, their loss, the fleetingness of life and the time together with loved ones. In such moments our best and deepest instincts may be revived from the dull thickness of everyday routine. Things come back into perspective. Worries over things that seemed like mountains shrink into the molehills that they really are. The big issues rise again, as they should, and we are given the chance to get our crooked lives and priorities straight. We learn again what really counts—family, friends, moments of life that we have taken for granted become pearls of great price. We "covet" them, the real treasure. All else fades. So it is if we are healthy and wise. But the two brothers were not wise men, they were fools. They squandered the rare moment of grief that could bind them. All they could think about was money. In their craving for security they had lost the real treasure of love. They had gained an inheritance, and lost their souls.

The brothers were not wrong to want an inheritance. They were wrong to "covet" it, to make it the end of their existence. So with the rich fool. He was not greedy simply because he desired a secure and pleasant retirement.[5] He was covetous, and foolish, because he believed that the storage of grain (IRAs and the rest) solved the problem of his human existence. When his building project was through, his *human* project was finished too. He had "arrived." He "had it made"— or so he believed. His life ended there, with the barns.

Had the story ended with the man's retirement, we would still sense the foolishness, the tragedy of his existence. There would still be a strange pathos about his merriment. That is because Jesus pictured him alone, totally alone—something utterly unthinkable for a rich person in that culture. No children run about the house, no wife or friends eat and drink with him. He sits and is "merry" all by himself. When he does speak, he speaks to himself. And when God speaks to him, the final question implies that the value of his treasure will perish with him. "And the things you have prepared, whose will they be?"

This parable sounds an alarm. It awakens us to a hard prophetic truth. Economic life makes us who we really are, forever. In Luke, Jesus stressed and repeated this truth so many times, in so many ways, that it is amazing how seldom we hear it in Christian churches and schools. The rich fool was an eternal fool, for he had stored no treasure in heaven. The word is not against solvency. But we must be very sure that our quest for solvency is animated by creative and redemptive love—for God and for the people in our lives. Too easily our productive work becomes an end unto itself—an idol—and financial success brings the strange paradox of poverty in our relationships. The parable reminds us that our relationships are the real tests of our success. They are the bottom line. They are the real treasure. It is a good time to ask ourselves honestly, are we rich or poor toward God? Are we wise, or are we fools in the things that matter most? The parable of the rich man and Lazarus puts this warning into sharp focus.

The Rich Man and Lazarus

In the sixteenth chapter of Luke the problem of economic identity comes to a head. The entire chapter consists of two parables about riches and the use of money that occur only in this Gospel. One is the story of the dishonest manager; the other is the tale of the rich man and Lazarus. In Luke's narrative, as will become clearer still, below, they are obviously linked in his mind to Jesus' encounters with the rich young ruler and Zacchaeus. They comment on the face-off between these two presentations of Jesus' commands. We shall first explore the story of the rich man and Lazarus, because it continues the negative theme of warning. We shall then proceed to the dishonest manager, which injects a theme of hope for the rich.[6]

Speaking to his disciples, Jesus began, "There was a rich man who was dressed in purple and fine linen and who feasted sumptuously every day." At his gate lay the poor man Lazarus, who was covered with sores. So wretched was he that scraps from the rich man's table were enough to satisfy him. Eventually the poor man died. The rich man also died. Here Jesus again makes another strike on the moral universe of his contemporaries, and perhaps of our own, shattering their expectations about the moral destiny of people. There is a great reversal of fortune and misfortune. When poor Lazarus died, the angels carried the man who had appeared accursed off to heaven, to rest in the very bosom of Abraham! After the rich man's burial, this man who had appeared to have a corner on God's favor found himself suffering torment in *hell,* separated from paradise by an abyss. Horrified, he pleaded with Abraham, saying, "Send Lazarus to dip the tip of his finger in water and cool my tongue." The irony of reversal had come full circle. The rich man now begged *Lazarus* for small relief. But Abraham was absolutely without mercy. He responded, "During your lifetime you received your good things, and Lazarus in like manner evil things; but now he is comforted here, and you are in agony." Turnabout, it seems, really is fair play.

Accepting his own fate, the rich man implored Abraham at least to send Lazarus to warn his five brothers, "so that they will not also come into this place of torment." But Abraham was still unmoved. "They have Moses and the prophets; they should listen to them." But the rich man, failing to grasp the force of this last statement, persisted. Surely if someone returned from the dead, they would listen. But Abraham was firm. "If they do not listen to Moses and the prophets, neither will they be convinced even if someone rises from the dead" (Lk 16:19-31).

What does this parable teach us? Its most obvious and puzzling feature is the great reversal. Some have suggested the simple, literal reading that God's plan for history is to turn everything upside down. The rich will become poor and the poor will become rich.[7] But this interpretation again implies that being rich is itself a damnable condition, and that being poor is a blessed one. We have explored the strongest objections to this view and need not repeat the arguments.[8] Furthermore, if just having good things in this life were damnable, then Abraham would be a poor judge. The very appearance of Abraham, who himself had some "good things" in his life, is provocative and suggests the presence of a deeper, more complex meaning.

What was wrong with the rich man, who is never even named? He did not exactly ignore Lazarus, for he knew him by name.[9] He had no doubt seen Lazarus hundreds of times by the gate to his house. It seems that he had tolerated this wretched presence for some length of time, and somehow (perhaps by arrangement) table scraps went outside so that Lazarus could, with the ceremonially unclean dogs who licked his sores, forage through the mess for meals. With this Lazarus was satisfied and asked for nothing more. The rich man could perhaps satisfy himself that the small kindness was better than nothing at all.

So what was damnable about the rich man? What should he have done? The answer, I believe, is in the words of Abraham. Twice he invoked the Old Testament to establish the just cause of punishment. "They have Moses and the prophets; they should listen to them." Whatever obligation he failed to meet, it was stated in Moses and the Prophets. Not only that, but it is in the most conspicuous *essence* of their writings. To have read the law and the Prophets is to have been warned—more clearly and powerfully than if someone returned from the dead.

The rich man had failed to adopt the exodus vision that we have explored. For this indeed was the essence of what the law and the Prophets urged on the rich in Israel. Moses and the Prophets obviously did not curse the rich just for being rich in an oppressed world. On the contrary, God blessed them with wealth and thus with lives of uncommon dominion and delight. This was good. But God also gave them uncommon obligations. They must represent the God of the exodus, the God in whom power and compassion embrace. Through compassion, the rich must enter into the world of the poor and must touch it with their liberating power. Like God, in their own ways they bring delight to the undelighted.

The rich man in our parable, however, entered daily through the wrong gate. He did not touch the world of Lazarus, nor was he touched by it. As the poor man lay in a hideous cloth heap, the rich man entered the gateway into his sumptuous world, and sat down every day in his purple linen to feast. As the dogs licked, and as Lazarus scavenged through his garbage outside, the rich man merrily gorged himself. In contrast, we think of Jesus' famous good Samaritan on the Jericho road who could not pass by the injured person. At risk to himself, and at considerable cost in money, time and trouble, he did whatever was needed to get the beaten man back on his feet. He was a good man, and he simply *could* not continue until something was done. But we imagine the rich man in our parable with a bounce in his step, never breaking his proud stride, perhaps even nodding at Lazarus, as he entered the gate. We imagine him humming to himself and chatting amiably with servants as he feasted. But as the food and wine were consumed and the merriment went on inside, the Lord of Israel looked down and grieved over Lazarus. In time, the scavenging cloth heap that was Lazarus became a mark of death on the rich man and his house.

The implication is that he ought to have helped Lazarus. But exactly how? By inviting him to dinner? By putting him up in a hospice until he was well again? By hiring him as a servant? Jesus never dictates the proper steps. He leaves that to our imaginations. The most important and basic thing is that we *hear* again the law and the Prophets and their exodus vision. The important thing is that we *try* to express it in our economic lives. There is no simple or single formula or checklist of rules to follow. It is more a matter of disposition. We *commit* ourselves to this vision, and we *reject* the serpentine way of the world, the way of self-absorbed oblivion and its lack of grieving.

But there is something more. For me, a very powerful feature of the story is the *nearness* of Lazarus. Lazarus was not "the beating crowd." He was not the global poor in the abstract. He was not even the poor of Israel, Jerusalem or Nazareth. He was Lazarus by the gate. Thus Jesus pictured the moral arena of our testing. Lazarus lay in a heap right on the rich man's doorway, and he lay there for some time, as part of the rich man's world. The rich man's moral responsibility and guilt arose from his *nearness*. This is something much deeper than mere physical or geographical proximity. Lazarus did not just happen to exist in the vicinity. In a more deeply existential way he entered into the rich man's realm and established a moral location there (quite possibly with the rich man's permission). The rich man's gate became his home, his "space" as a human being. And he was the real "gate" of testing for his master. Moral location generates moral conditions and moral obligations.

The rich man was not condemned for failing outright to fight poverty throughout the Roman and Palestinian political realms, for he was not called to be the Messiah, nor the emperor, nor even a prince. No, he was judged by the standard of Lazarus. For he was called to hear the groaning of his people, to come near to them, and to use his power to set them free. To put this in the language of Old Testament metaphor, we have seen that when God blesses people with riches, he gives them dominion over a realm and freedom for delight. But dominion and freedom are limited by responsibilities and obligations, especially to the poor in their realms. This idea of realms and responsibilities over them begins in Genesis with the creation of human beings in the image of God. It unfolds in diverse ways throughout the Law, the Prophets and the writings of Wisdom. Now we have it in a new form in the narrative world of Jesus' story. The wealthy man had been given charge over a realm where he must represent God—the God of power, compassion and delight. Like this man, Jesus suggests, God's people are judged within the boundaries of their realms.

The notions of "nearness" and "realms" thus stress the responsibilities of the rich. But they also suggest a truth that those who preach prophetic messages of responsibility often miss. Scripture indeed makes it clear that our freedoms as rich people are limited by great obligations. But it also implies that our obligations are not infinite either. They are graciously limited by the nature of the freedom for a good life, which is God's gift to us. The obligation of the rich to redeem the poor (which limits our freedom for delight) is itself limited by God's gracious blessing on our freedom to be what he created us to be. First, we are mere creatures, not gods. Second, we are creatures made for lives of royal dominion, dignity and delight. The most intense Christian moralists (and the most sensitive souls who hear them) are prone to forget both. The peculiar nature of our creatureliness limits our realm of freedom *and* responsibility. God calls us to be no more and no less than what we are. We dare not act like gods in either direction. The rich man failed to grasp the limitations on his freedom; but sensitive people may fail in the other extreme. They (we) may not fully grasp the graciousness of the God who judges us. He judges us within boundaries.[10]

The idea of "nearness" suggests that our obligations are strongest, and our moral tests most severe, where they are nearest. Of course "nearness" will mean something different for each person and moral situation. We cannot do justice to the subject here. But "nearness" will mean one thing to a teacher, another to a banker and quite another to a professional politician, a husband, a housewife, a truck driver or a garbage collector. Most of us have several callings or "realms" with different sets of freedoms and obligations, boundaries and limits. We must sort them out individually, and often quite intuitively. "Nearness" has a dimension of the spiritual or psychological. The cause of freedom in Russia may be "near" to my grandfather, even though he emigrated to America long ago. A loved one may be "near" even though she has moved to a distant land. Different "nearnesses" will create their own peculiar kinds of obligations for appropriate kinds of action. These actions may range from empathic prayer to political lobbying to miles of hard travel for a cause. A whole volume could be written on the idea of nearness and on the notion of callings as boundaried realms.

But in general terms, to apply the metaphor to ourselves, these ideas mean that each of us needs a clear vision of our unique realm and its boundaries. This is crucial to knowing our real obligations—

and freedoms. The question becomes, What does it mean to live appropriately, in both freedom and compassion, in any given realm of life? The parable strongly suggests something about where to begin: at our own doorstep. There is the nearness of our own bodies and souls, the nearness of our spouses and children, our parents, friends and relatives. There is the nearness of work, our clients, employers and employees. This movement continues outward to communities—our town, county, state and nation.

However, let us not be little messiahs as we move outward. We must have a spirituality of our own creatureliness and of God's grace. God does not normally require that we move outward in economic life beyond our capacities for productive action and delight in life. Messianic crusading can do terrible damage to ourselves, our loved ones and our witness in the world. It is often anxiety and desperation (or even arrogance) transparently masquerading as faith and love.

Our obligations are finite, just as we are. We will struggle unto death for absolute clarity about the boundaries, the range and the limits of our freedoms and obligations. But God, as the psalmist wrote, "knows we are dust." He calls us to *try*—not to be crushed. To again cite the poet Eliot, "For us there is only the trying, the rest is not our business."

The Dishonest Manager
Jesus told the parable of the dishonest manager to his disciples (Lk 16:1). However, others must have gathered around to hear it, because Luke reports that some Pharisees were within earshot and laughed at Jesus's concluding lesson: "You cannot serve God and wealth" (Lk 16:13). In fact, this ridicule prompted him to tell the parable of the rich man and Lazarus—it was for their primary benefit. Luke notes that the Pharisees were not only lovers of piety but also "lovers of money." To them Jesus gave harsh images of a reputable rich man suffering in hell because of his wrongful use of money. In contrast, the story of the dishonest manager is about a disreputable fellow who

redeems himself through his right use of wealth. The stories thus operate in tandem to create a moment of crisis and choice for rich people.[11]

Jesus began, "There was a rich man who had a manager, and charges were brought to him that this man was squandering his property." When the rich man discovered this, he fired him. Facing poverty, the manager wondered fearfully about his future. "What will I do . . . ? I am not strong enough to dig, and I am ashamed to beg." Not one to give up easily, he devised a plan. "I have decided what to do so that, when I am dismissed as manager, people may welcome me into their homes." The manager made his old rounds and allowed people to write off portions of their debts—as much as fifty percent. Jesus ended the parable. "His master commended the dishonest manager because he had acted shrewdly; for the children of this age are more shrewd in dealing with their own generation than are the children of light" (Lk 16:1-8).

Some of Jesus' best-known teachings about wealth arose on this occasion.

> I tell you, make friends for yourselves by means of dishonest wealth so that when it is gone, they may welcome you into the eternal homes. Whoever is faithful in a very little is faithful also in much; and whoever is dishonest in a very little is dishonest also in much. (Lk 16:9-10)

He exhorted his disciples to ponder this connection. "If then you have not been faithful with the dishonest wealth, who will entrust to you the true riches?" (Lk 16:11). This was also the occasion for his now-famous words: "No slave can serve two masters; for a slave will either hate the one and love the other, or be devoted to the one and despise the other. You cannot serve God and wealth" (Lk 16:13). And, as noted, the Pharisees "ridiculed him" (Lk 16:14).

One of the most puzzling features of this parable is Jesus' approval of the dishonest manager. Recent scholarship may shine some light on the problem. In the ancient world, managers commonly loaned their *own* money to clients on the side, so that a portion of the debt was typically owed to them.[12] If Jesus presumed this convention, then the manager's dishonesty was in the dealings that got him fired, not in canceling the debts. This would instead make his actions seem remarkably shrewd, which is the point of the story. The prospect of unemployment might have sent him into a panic about solvency, and he well might have called in his debts. But then what? With no income, the well would soon run dry, and the embittered former debtors would have rejoiced. The moment of anxiety would have launched him into an isolated, friendless existence in poverty. But the manager did not let fear cloud his mind. By canceling the debts (and thus making himself penniless) he ingeniously created a wealth of "friends" who would receive him into their houses. Thus his old master "commended" him for his cunning, and we may imagine that he got his old job back.

The man in the story is for us a model of prudence on a cosmic scale, because he used his position of power in a doubly redemptive way. First, by not falling into self-contained fear, he had faith enough to free himself to liberate others, and so he redeemed himself. It is a renewed form of the old vision. By opening up in faith and courage to liberate others, rich people liberate themselves and find salvation. And there is no indication in the parable (in spite of common opinion on the subject) that this is at all a bad motive. Jesus' words of explanation stress that the rich must be very concerned about their *own* salvation, and that this comes, ironically, through our actions to save others. We "make friends" with "dishonest wealth." Money, even that which originates through morally dubious channels, becomes integral to God's and our work of reconciliation and redemption.

In the parable Jesus made the prophetic connection between economic life and eternal life about as straightforward as it could be.[13] He told the disciples bluntly that if they are not "faithful with the dishonest wealth," they cannot expect to inherit "the true riches." The point of making friends with "dishonest wealth" is essential to attaining "eternal homes." We should not presume that Jesus meant that money was simply evil. For then it would have been evil for Jesus to have it, and very strange for him to advise people to use it to "gain friends." It must rather be a cryptic way of injecting a note of realism. As money flows through the economic systems of the world, like a river, it will inevitably pick up pollutants along the way. But (so Jesus implied) this must not stop us from putting the system to redemptive uses. In fact he commands us to do so. For the rich, courage and faithfulness in the realm of money is the measure of our faithfulness to God. Money may not be our "master," but it must be our "servant" in bringing release to people. Hence we serve God.

But what is faithfulness in this context? True faithfulness displays itself in a disposition of freedom from anxiety. It has to do with the organizing principles and values that shape our identities. In the critical moment, the manager does not hunker down, horde his wealth and hide from the world. He rather bravely and shrewdly opens up, and in his nefarious manner *gives* himself to others, and others thus give themselves to him. And as with Zacchaeus, it also has to do with converting the dark, oppressive powers of the world system ("dishonest wealth") into powers for creation and redemption. So the kingdom comes through the rich. And as with the rich man and Lazarus, the notion of nearness enters in. The manager's moment of moral trial, testing and triumph was framed by the small boundaries of his job as a money manager. The larger world system of "dishonest wealth" fades. Nothing remotely like the scrupulous "principle of guilt by implication in fallen structures" comes into play. The real world of moral life is the little group of people locked in the grip of debt and entirely at his mercy. When people are drowning, you do not waste time analyzing the pollution levels of the water. What really matters is that the conniving manager brought a brand new life and integrity to that depressed little world. His courageous, creative action converted it into a community of redemption for everyone. How much more integrity and life should the children of light bring to their worlds!

The Parable of the Ten Pounds

As we have seen, the story of Zacchaeus (Jesus' last encounter with a rich person) brings a gracious resolution of the dreadful tension that Luke's Jesus created in the souls of rich Christians. The way into the kingdom for Zacchaeus is not the way of poverty. Salvation comes to his house through creative and redemptive uses of his economic power. Luke obviously placed the parable of the ten pounds to be read while we are still recovering from the shock of Jesus and Zacchaeus. "As they were listening to this, he went on to tell a parable" (Lk 19:11). The parable of the ten pounds thus reaffirms and expands the lessons of Zacchaeus. Luke also explains that Jesus told the story "because he was near Jerusalem, and because they supposed that the kingdom of God was to appear immediately" (Lk 19:11). Of course they were wrong. Jesus was to die, and there would be a time "between the times," during which the kingdom comes but is not yet consummated in its fullness. This is the time when servants of the king must live in faith without the fullness of his presence. It is the time of testing—both for the world and for ourselves. The parable thus comes at a crucial place in the Gospel.[14] It is our last vision of faithfulness in economic life, in the absence of our Lord, until the kingdom finally comes.[15]

So began the story. "A nobleman went to a distant country to get royal power for himself and then return." The nobleman gave each of his ten servants a pound to "do business with" until he came back.[16] When he returned the nobleman asked each servant to give an account of what he had done. The first servant had turned the one pound into ten. In words that connect the story with the parable of the dishonest manager, the master commended him: "Well done, good slave! Because you have been trustworthy in a very small thing, take charge of ten cities.'"[17] The second servant had parlayed his pound into five, and so the master gave him rule over *five* cities. But the third servant had hidden his pound in a cloth. He excused himself, saying, "I was afraid of you, because you are a harsh man; you take what you did not deposit, and reap what you did not sow."

At this the nobleman became furious and condemned the man out of his own mouth. "You knew, did you, that I was a harsh man, taking what I did not deposit and reaping what I did not sow? Why then did you not put my money into the bank? Then when I returned, I could have collected it with interest." He then instructed the other servants to take the man's pound and give it to the man who had ten. Sensing their wonderment, he explained the hard truth. "I tell you, to all those who have, more will be given; but from those who have nothing, even what they have will be taken away." The master then commanded them to bring his enemies before him, those "who did not want me to be king over them," and to slay them (Lk 19:11-27).

The parable delivers another blow to our predictable moral universe. Seeming to demolish the Old Testament vision, the "radical Jesus" had come cursing the rich and blessing the poor. But we have learned that he did not come to destroy Moses and the Prophets. He came to fulfill them in the new age of his own coming. The parable of the ten pounds is the last act in this creative process from strength to weakness and back to strength. Not much in Christian theology today honors God as a warrior-king, or honors the courage of godly people in the marketplace. But this is a parable of power and the enlargement of dominion through wealth. It is a parable that honors the fearsome courage and strength of a warrior and king who will not stop until his realm is enlarged over all the earth. It is a parable that honors the strength and courage of his servants who are fruitful in the worldly realms of power. It is a parable that honors the *enlargement* of people who would become stronger, and would make their master stronger, through the creation of wealth. And it is also a parable of dire warning against a spirit of timidity and fruitlessness in our response to the economic world.

The two praiseworthy servants create a most interesting picture of faithfulness. More to the point, they create a most provocative image of the master whom they serve. Although he is away for most of it, his spirit dominates the whole parable. He is a powerful figure, a man of fierce "enlargement." This, I believe, is the right metaphor for understanding and applying the whole story. Unlike Zacchaeus and the dishonest manager (or the negative lessons of Lazarus and the rich man), virtue for the two servants is not connected with an obligation to empower the poor. It is rather about their obligation to enter the world and to enlarge the master's power and dominion within it while he is away. He has gone to take a kingdom; this defines the spirit in which *they* must serve him. They must be the kind of people with whom a warrior-king can identify and of whom he can be proud, and this they are. In the small matter of the pound, they have proved themselves worthy of greatness.

But what about the servant who has failed? We are familiar with Jesus' many warnings about the dangers of wealth and success. With this person, however, Jesus sounds a very different alarm, one that is missing from moral theology today. He warns against being so conscious of our master's severity that our economic lives become fruitless. The servant's excuse sounded pious. (It was of the "O-lord-thou-art-so-great-and-I-am-nothing" variety.)[18] But in truth he was a coward who could not take the stresses of responsibility in the world of business.

The true servant of a warrior-king cannot be a coward. A little heartburn and fatigue will not stop him from putting on the armor every morning, going to the office and doing his best to win the day in his small world. Most professionals will understand this immediately. The economic world is a field of "war," and it takes wit, bravery and a strong will that is loath to surrender if they are to compete—and win—for what is right. The moral leadership of the church does not understand this. In my whole life I have never once heard (nor heard of) a sermon on the dangers of cowardice in the business world, much less on the virtues of bravery competing within it. "Warrior theology" seems to have been left somewhere back in the Middle Ages. But the parable (in its context) is a strong warning against those who would erode the strong, aggressive, competitive spirit of economic (and not only that) behavior among Christians who believe that their king has given them pounds to put to work until he comes. Let us beware lest we find ourselves aging adolescents, hiding lives of failed escapism behind a thin veil of pious excuses, while the king gives his cities to the strong.

Quite obviously, Jesus did not pronounce an unqualified blessing on economic gain. His life and teachings all demonstrate the conditions for godliness that must exist before our gains become true "enlargement" in his kingdom. However, if those conditions have been recreated, then the creative, productive economic life becomes something that is absolutely true to our humanity and to the identity of God. For people who have good reason to believe that God has blessed and entrusted them with wealth and the ability to create it, creative and productive economic living is both a mandate and a blessing. They should view it as good, and so should the moral leadership of the church. There comes a time in the lives of such people when agonizing over imagined guilt and the Lord's displeasure drags on into nothing more than glorified diffidence, sanctimonious fear. Having done what they can to satisfy the conditions, committing themselves to lives of servant-dominion, professional people must begin to cultivate a spirituality of royal confidence in the goodness of their calling. Jesus tells us to be brave.

This reaches all the way back to the creation mandate and blessing to "be fruitful and multiply, and fill the earth and subdue it." After all the requisite qualifications have been made, that is essentially what human life is all about. The parable again blesses fruitfulness in the economic realm.[19]

One last feature in Luke's version of the parable deserves a few words. The servants enlarged a very small amount of money, but the master gave them whole cities in return. There is a logic of disproportionate gain here. It strongly suggests a connection between faithful enlargement in this life and greater enlargement in the life to come. This is the twist on the connection between economic life and eternal life that we found in the Wisdom writings.

The parable (and its logic of disproportionality) calls us back to the metaphor of "realms." It may seem a small thing that God has made us what we are. Most people, even professionals, feel that they are ultimately insignificant, that their work does not really matter. The parable of the ten pounds, however, dignifies the small kingdom and its small queen or king. It suggests that the real treasure of human history is hidden in ordinary people enlarging realms that hardly seem great. C. S. Lewis once wrote that a charwoman, carrying out her duties faithfully, may become, in the kingdom of God, a creature of such glory that kings would be tempted to worship her.

The message, I believe, is to enlarge and to dignify whatever realm God has given us. We should go about our work with royal pride and dignity, not with the tackiness that is so prevalent in our culture. The church should be a people with class. The essence of life is not in the quantity and visibility of our dominion, but in its quality. This only the nobleman truly knows, and he will reward our labors as only he can. By his grace, there is eternal glory buried within the passing smallness of Christian lives. The teacher, the doctor, the lawyer, the insurance agent, the small motel manager, the fry cook, the owner of the toy store, the professional athlete, the school janitor, the film actress or actor, the hardware merchant, the corporate executive or college administrator—great or small—all have "pounds" to put to work with royal grace, purpose and effect. Such servants befit the warrior and king of the universe whom they serve.

9

LIFESTYLES OF THE RICH & FAITHFUL IN THE EARLY CHURCH

They would sell their possessions and goods.
ACTS 2:45

*A*ll the great acts of God were "economic" events. The creation of the material world and its delights, the liberation of Israel from slavery to freedom, their exile back into bondage and the incarnate life of Jesus Christ all were explosions of God's economic vision for the earth. So was the creation of the church. The coming of the Holy Spirit on the day of Pentecost created a new community of fresh economic life.

Again we must depend on Luke for our vision of the event. In the book of Acts he records that a sound came from heaven "like the rush of a violent wind" (Acts 2:2). Tongues of fire rested on the company of followers (about 120 of them), and they suddenly began to speak in the many languages that divided them—the awful day of great Babel was done. At the end of this new day, about three thousand souls had repented and committed themselves to the cause of Christ (Acts 2:41).

But the wonders of the Spirit did not confine themselves to invisible "spiritual" realms. The most visible mark of the new community was the miraculous transformation of its economic life. Luke records that the new believers "were together and had all things in common; they would sell their possessions and goods and distribute the proceeds to all, as any had need" (Acts 2:44-45). This visible display of new life sealed their words with the stamp of truth, and so "the Lord added to their number" (Acts 2:47).

The picture is no doubt idealized, as ancient history always was, but we must not detach it from Luke's original purpose in writing what was once Luke-Acts: "to set down an orderly account" of things "just as they were handed on to us by those who from the beginning were eyewitnesses" (Lk 1:1-4).[1] The biblical Christian must take it seriously as an event in redemptive history with real economic implications for the present.

We are told that the first believers were "of one heart and soul" (Acts 4:32), a spiritual reality that became visible. Luke writes that "no one claimed private ownership of any possessions, but everything they owned was held in common" (Acts 4:32). The moral vision and purpose that guided them was evident in the outcome of their actions: "there was not a needy person among them" (Acts 4:34). Nor did they eliminate poverty with an ancient world's parallel to our "bake sales." The richest Christians immediately liquidated some of their largest and most valuable assets. Luke writes, "for as many as owned *lands* or *houses* sold them and brought the proceeds of what was sold. They laid it at the apostles' feet, and it was distributed to each as any had need" (Acts 4:34-35; italics mine).

There is of course a thicket of debates around these texts. What kind of economic system was this? Did the first Christians abolish private property? Did the Jerusalem church "decapitalise, communalise, and come to rely on the financial support of foreigners"?? And, whatever it was and whether it was a failure or a success, just how does the experiment in Jerusalem apply to the universal church, especially in the modern world? Does it have an application to the larger national economies of the world? We will seek our way through this thicket as best we can. But whatever the exact mechanisms and applications of the "Jerusalem experiment," one thing is clear. Rich Christians immediately knew and accepted the special role they had to play. They invented the remarkable practice of what we may call economic evangelism. It is a role that only the rich can play.

The Jerusalem church had drunk deeply from the waters of the Old Testament (we remember that they were first of all Jews), and they had listened to Jesus. They knew better than to spiritualize their faith. No one had to persuade them that proclaiming the gospel was an economic event. They understood the vision: flourishing in the body, especially among the poor, was the sign of God's victorious liberation of the spirit. So it was in Jerusalem. For them it was simply a given that the church must free its members from poverty. The gospel was not really "heard" until the strongholds that deprived people of decent food, clothing, shelter and simple human delight were broken. And so, by the rich and faithful, the poor were set free. Like ghostly shades from Jerusalem's vast economic underworld, they came into the light of this Christian morning. Resurrected from living death in poverty, they arose as new creatures with new bodies. And they came to the table that Jesus had prepared for them. The angels must have wept for joy.

Some have missed the point, however. This is not so much a story of the poor and their liberation as it is about the rich and their role as liberators. For some of us lifetime pew sitters the scene is difficult to imagine. Rich Christians made the church into a place of awesome power for good. Because of them the little ones who gathered there found freedom and life as nowhere else. The Jerusalem church was a place of joy and celebration. Luke describes their gatherings in the language of banqueting and delight. He writes that they "broke bread at home and ate their food with glad and generous hearts" (Acts 2:46). Through economic evangelism the lives of desperate people were filled by the fullness of Christ's kingdom. And the lives of the rich were crowned by the power and compassion of their liberating actions. They identified themselves with God, the Servant-Lord, and he thus identified with them. It was the vision of creation and exodus all over again, in concentrated, Christlike form.

Luke suggests that this economic evangelism had yet another effect. Against enormous odds, including the public perception that Jesus had destroyed the law, the actions of rich Christians commanded the people's respect. By playing their role faithfully, rich Christians dramatically portrayed the true character of Jesus Christ to a hard and skeptical crowd—the very people who had rejected and crucified him. The performance was a convincing triumph: "day by day the Lord added to their number" (Acts 2:47). What a contrast to our present cultural situation! Today, outsiders are given the ugly face of self-serving evil that they associate with televangelists, who, when they are not being reprimanded for sexual immorality or indicted for public fraud, seem to spend more time on the air asking for money than anything else. In Jerusalem the rich stood out as brave liberators, and their reward, at least in the critical beginning, was a good deal of public trust. In the lives of the rich, the world saw the incarnation of powerful goodness. This was compelling stuff. The lesson is that when powerful people act they make a powerful impression. It is difficult to ignore the dinosaur in the garden. Likewise, when they act badly, the damage is very great. But, again, as the character of Ebenezer Scrooge has taught us now for decades, almost nothing moves us more to suspect the work of higher powers than the transformation of a selfish rich person into a mighty force for good.

Christian Communism?

Rich Christians are thus blessed with the obligation to practice "economic evangelism" before a doubting world. But here more troublesome questions arise. Rich Christians are to give and to liberate, but just how are we to organize ourselves and to live? Exactly what were the economic mechanisms of this experiment in Jerusalem? And what principles emerge from Luke's narrative that are binding on our economic lives today?

Some Christian writers believe that the New Testament economic principles were those of decapitalization and communalism.[3] Art Gish writes bluntly that "Private property is abolished." By application, he judges that "as Christians we need to make a complete break with the capitalist economy."[4] The book of Acts in particular, and Scripture in general, teaches that "capitalism stands opposed to koinonia," according to Gish.[5] Barry Gordon also understands Luke's theological vision as communal and thus in favor of decapitalization among Christians. However, with others he views this as a failed experiment—for two reasons. First, the Jerusalem church, without asset protection, became vulnerable to economic crises. With bad weather came economic devastation. Within the decade Jerusalem—the place of Christ's visible triumph over poverty—had became a welfare church. Second, research proves (notwithstanding the claims made by Gish and others) that, for whatever reason, churches outside of Jerusalem did not follow its example of disinvestment and communalism. Thus, they cannot have viewed its principles and exact mechanisms as the norm.[6]

Very serious problems arise with both applications: either we discard our whole economic system, or we discard the authority of Acts 2 and 4 over our economic life. However, it is not at all clear from Luke's account that this *was* an experiment with principles of disinvestment and communalism. The remarkable story of Barnabas, Ananias and Sapphira gives the most detailed impression of the mechanisms, and it clearly reveals that the system respected personal freedom and control over property. This was not clearly a model of decapitalization or disinvestment, but something else.

In this story of economic good and evil, perhaps purposely reminding readers of the similar story of Achan in Joshua,[7] Luke presents Barnabas as a godly man who "sold a field that belonged to him, then brought the money, and laid it at the apostles' feet" (Acts 4:37). Ananias and Sapphira next seem to follow his good example. They also sold a piece of property and presented the money to the apostles. Only, we are told, they "kept back some of the proceeds" and brought *only a part* of it to the apostles (Acts 5:1-2). Peter confronted them, and (apart from whatever historical or moral objections we may have about the episode as recorded) we must note the economic principles of his moral argument and accusation. He could not excuse them, since before the property was sold, "did it not remain your own? And after it was sold, were not the proceeds at your disposal?" (Acts 5:4).

In Peter's line of argument we thus learn that earlier statements about having "all things in common" did not mean abolishing private property or setting up communal mechanisms of ownership.[8] As scholar F. F. Bruce puts it, "No compulsion had been laid on Ananias to sell his property."[9] On the contrary, the church carefully honored the rights and freedoms of people (here a family) over their property at every step in the process. First, the decision to sell land was completely voluntary. No moral principle (neither communalistic nor utilitarian) against owning and holding property was in force. Neither was there any system of moral intimidation or guilt manipulation. Second, even after the sale, the profits remained under the sellers' final control for distribution. The implication is that they did not *have* to give it all to the apostles. Their sin was not in withholding part of the profits, but rather in claiming that they gave everything when they had done nothing of the kind. In fact, as Peter implies, it was the voluntary nature of the system that made their action so very reprehensible. The sin was not that they were selfish capitalists, but that they were liars and hypocrites. They pretended to be something that they were not, and deceit is a cancer in the church. Because their privacy and dignity had been respected, there was no excuse for their behavior, no place for them in the church. The Lord would strike them dead, which Luke says he did, and the bodies were carried off to the ground.

Utilitarian Living?

Citing the same features of the story, even the countercultural Ron Sider rightly agrees that the church "did not insist on absolute economic equality. Nor did they abolish private property."[10] But for Sider, the working principle, while not communal or communistic, was utilitarian. The key was not the evils of owning property, but the existence of *needs* created by the misfortune of *not* owning property. Sider focuses on Luke's statement "they would sell their possessions and goods and distribute the proceeds to all, *as any had need*" (Acts 2:45; italics mine). Most will agree with Sider's larger point, I hope, that the system was not communistic and that the rich were (and are) challenged by a model of redemptive living to meet the needs of poor Christians as they arise.[11]

But we can approach people's needs through very different patterns of moral reasoning. Sider's reasoning comports with what I have called utilitarian reasoning throughout this book. That is in essence the view that enjoyment of superfluous wealth is morally wrong in a context where others have unsatisfied basic needs. Utilitarianism is, and must be, always suspicious of what we have called delight. And if there is a place in Scripture where the utilitarian position might find warrant for the Christian, it is here, in Acts.

But there is much against the utilitarian reading. First, practical reasons—what we might call the ethical field of utilitarianism—ought to make anyone skeptical. If our job mainly is to meet needs as they arise, exactly how are we to live as economic persons? With this question, the utilitarian obviously steps off into very deep waters. For as I argued earlier, human need is a bottomless, endless abyss of possible obligations. And our own needs are difficult, perhaps impossible, to define with the confidence that we are not fooling ourselves, rationalizing, for example, that we really need two cars—or even one? What good excuse could there possibly be for taking a college degree that costs forty or fifty thousand dollars at a private liberal arts college, when one can get perfectly serviceable degrees for much less at public institutions?

The point here is that, when we adopt utilitarian principles, we must also adopt an absolute obsession with moral justification—with justifying every action that involves us in consumption. Which is to say that, in our global economy with its flood of mass information about the world's needs, we must become obsessed with the justification of our nearly every action. It is rather like the older philosophers who thought that every single belief must be thoroughly justified before we can hold it confidently as truth. But it is now well known that this system of belief justification generated worn-out relativists more than it did forceful believers in the truth.[12] It is very hard to see how anyone trying rigorously to act in this ethical field could ever develop the moral conviction needed for strong assertion and moral leadership in the culture.

Another difficulty with utilitarianism is with its coherence as a strategy for liberation. J. Du Pont's statement on Christian poverty is widely quoted by liberationists: "If goods are held in common, it is not therefore in order to become poor for love of an ideal of poverty; rather it is so that there will be no more poor. The ideal pursued is, once again, charity, a true love for the poor."[13]

The story in Acts is indeed deeply hostile to economic poverty, as is the entire Bible. However, when Sider, Gutiérrez, Du Pont and others demand that Christians become poor to the point of having no excess, in order to eliminate poverty on a global scale, we simply must protest. To whatever extent we become poorer we create degrees of poverty and (in one fashion or another) we foster the powerlessness that comes with being poor. Oddly, by so identifying with weakness, we reduce our power to liberate, and we thus lose our capacity to identify ourselves with the liberating power of God. But this power is our only real source of hope that liberation is more than just a "pocketful of promises," to quote from Paul Simon's "The Boxer." If my cup is not full, I cannot very well help to fill the empty cups of my friends. "Liberation" in modern theology describes an event of power whereby the rich use power to destroy poverty and to empower the poor. But if that event also destroys the condition of being rich, then the power to liberate (and to sustain the conditions of liberation) is thereby lost.[14]

The practical problem is exemplified by the life of John Wesley, whom Sider holds up as a model for rich Christians. Wesley believed that Christians must give away all but "the plain necessaries of life." He was neither a communist nor a socialist. He understood that we need enough capital to perform our calling or business.[15] But Wesley judged that a Christian who takes more than these plain necessaries "lives in an open, habitual denial of the Lord" and has gained "riches and hell-fire."[16] Aware that only wealth can liberate from poverty, he conceded that Christians in business ought to keep productive capital, so that they might continue to create wealth for the greater good of the poor.[17] But he stressed that Christians must give all "excess" profits to others, beginning with the greatest "need." True to his principles, Wesley rigorously did this himself.

However, a recent essay that is mainly sympathetic with his economic life also discloses some pretty disturbing facts.[18] Wesley was absolutely committed to giving away all but the necessaries, which he did. But one day a terrible fire destroyed the Wesley home. The family did not have the financial resources to recover. As a direct consequence of his policies (which forbade personal investment savings), his seven children and three sisters lived the rest of their lives in debt. By their own bitter testimonies this left deep emotional scars. They felt themselves sacrificial victims on the stone altar of Wesley's "calling from God" to save everyone but his own.

I do not question John Wesley's motives. Undoubtedly they were meant for good. But I find it very difficult not to regard his behavior in economic life as confused and tragic. He looked at the Christian economic life and saw almost only obligations. For all his well-known principles and rigor, he somehow missed the biblical vision of personal freedom, delight and blessing. He lacked the closely connected intuition of "nearness" that forms boundaries around our zeal and protects us and those around us from our own messianic tendencies.[19] The man whose goal in life was to free people from poverty thereby impoverished his own family. I do not see how utilitarianism can escape from the shadows of this kind of paradox without really denying its own principles, or qualifying itself to death.

Our primary question is not whether utilitarianism makes good common sense or is a coherent strategy in practice, but whether its way of reasoning is biblical. In earlier chapters we have seen good reasons throughout Scripture against thinking so. From a certain perspective, the Bible is actually quite antagonistic to it. The biblical vision, from Genesis to Jesus Christ, goes against its whole spirit and cast of mind. The main problem is that utilitarianism damages the vision of human dignity, dominion and delight that Scripture so passionately protects. As we have seen throughout the sacred story, even in the suffering life of Jesus, God protected his basic human dignity by blessing him and his followers with what utilitarians count as "superfluous" things. The end point of redemption in its fullest form is not mere survival, but delightful and compassionate dominion.

Our obligations to the poor do not arise from a strict system of "need," but from this vision of royal abundance in life and from discerning awareness of the needs that arise with a kind of compelling nearness, within the boundaries of our calling and realm as God has established them. Compassion moves the soul to wish such delight for all people, and to know that it is good in the sense of the created structure of the world itself. And it inspires us to work with God toward that end, to "seek his kingdom" in that way. That is why our obligations to the poor do not erase God's blessing on our delight. In truth, our obligations very much depend on this blessing. They instruct us to determine how to bring freedom and dignity to our poor "neighbors." This vision of blessing and duty fiercely protects all human beings, rich and poor, from relentless powers that would reduce human life in this world to a joyless human feedlot, where every beast, to use Lear's image, has just enough to keep it alive. That would not be "good," as Genesis uses the term; it would be alienation from life, a form of death.

God has formed boundaries that protect human delight. But utilitarianism erodes these boundaries and the human spirit enters into a night of demons whispering. As we have observed, by necessity every pleasure must be subjected to a thousand courts. Nothing "superfluous" can ever justify itself. We can never clear ourselves of guilt for enjoying even the slightest luxury. Where Scripture blesses us with the lightness of freedom to rejoice, give thanks and enjoy good things, we are haunted by a pitilessly accusing conscience. Christianity shrinks into a fetal ball—something like what Garrison Keillor must have had in mind when he whimsically invented for Lake Wobegon a church named "Our Lady of Perpetual Responsibility." It might have been any number of Protestant names. Before we adopt without pause the utilitarian reading of Acts, we must ask, Is this life of obsessive self-justification, moral ambivalence, guilt and diffidence the spiritual vision of the Christian life that Christ came to bring? Is this at all consonant with the great theme of God's justification of people, by grace, which sets them free from the law? Is this the vision of life that we mean to tell non-Christians, especially those in the professions, that they can look forward to, if only they repent and believe? But we must return more specifically to Acts. It may at first seem a strange claim to make, but I believe that this important document, in its own peculiar way, sustains the biblical vision of compassionate dominion and delight that has emerged in various forms throughout our search through the Scriptures. I believe that Sider unintentionally weakens his own utilitarian interpretation when he reasons thus: " 'No one said that any of the things which he possessed was his own.' That does not mean that everyone donated everything. Later in Acts we see that John Mark's mother, Mary, still owned her house (12:12). Others undoubtedly also retained some private property."[20]

Notice what he implies here. People kept possessions, and it would be presumptuous to insist that they kept only "the plain necessaries." In that culture owning homes was more a luxury than a strict necessity. This is in fact a premise in the utilitarian argument—by liquidating homes, the first Christians modeled the practice of giving away the extras. The text simply does not tell us how much people gave away in proportion to what they had, nor what they did with the rest. It tells us that Barnabas sold a field to meet needs. It does not tell us whether or not he owned other fields, or how he lived ever after. We do not know. The text does not follow him home and track him down to see if his activities in the kitchen, the sitting room, bathroom or work place were politically or environmentally correct according to utilitarian norms in an age of scarcity and suffering. What it does teach is that the rich made heroic sacrifices to eliminate poverty in the church, that they were strategically successful at this, that the impact for good was very, very great, both within and outside of the church, and God was pleased by their works.

Nor did the church itself quite behave in a utilitarian manner in its use and distribution of the money given to them by the rich. For one thing, they did not at all go by the strict table of societal need. It seems that a limiting and liberating principle of "nearness" and "boundaries" was in operation. The darkest lines of obligation in the text are drawn around the community of Christians, with not a trace of moral panic about the world outside, the global poor. The streets of Jerusalem were swarming with homeless people of every imaginable sort. It was a place of desperation. In the face of this immense need, how could wealthy Christians justify expending resources solely on members of the church? But this is what they did. It is similar to what we observed in the laws of ancient Israel, where the primary (not the sole) obligations, by God's mercy, all but ended with the boundaries of the nation. Here was the new Israel, a new realm of primary obligations.

The rich Christians were not called to a system based on strict need, but rather to one that was bounded by the needs that arose within a realm of nearness, where freedom and delight might abound in degrees for everyone. By concentrating on needs within that limited realm, they could become powerful liberators without destroying their power to liberate. Obviously, they also had obligations to their immediate families, employees and friends. And they had the normal duties that go with citizenry and special callings of a dozen kinds. But again the text wisely suggests, in part by its silence on these matters, that knowing our creaturely limits and freedoms is essential to liberating people in the right way.

Luke also notes that the new church was itself a place of celebration and delight. As we saw, he stresses that the first gatherings were more like feasts than like some of our contemporary somber services. They mirrored the banquets of Christ's kingdom. Occasionally they gathered in homes where they ate and drank together in good cheer, as the disciples had done with Jesus. But the strict utilitarian mind cannot freely partake of such extravagance in the face of such need. It rather sings with the modern hymn, "So long as pain and strife remain, we will not rejoice or celebrate." The remaining homes should be sold, the rest given to the poor. At best, the freedom to celebrate

celebrate is a crippled one.

In sum, the Jerusalem experiment is not a model for principled communism or for serious utilitarianism. It is rather a model of liberation and freedom that hearkens images of exodus theology and its vision (and perhaps with flashes of light from the jubilee) for people who expressed their blessed richness in liberating godliness. It highlights the great obligations of the rich to identify with God as the liberator of the poor. But its limiting principles of individual freedom over property, nearness and boundaried realms of obligation also protect the vision of dignity, dominion and delight that is the essence of liberation and life for all human beings. The story of Jerusalem thus obliges and blesses rich Christians. It blesses and burdens us with the role of Christ, the King of liberation and royal delight, in the church and on the stage of the world. If we are seeking a more controlled and clearer guidance system than this, I do not think we will find it in the sacred story. And the fact that Christians throughout the empire, from very early on, felt intuitively free to apply these principles in very different ways from what Luke pictures in Acts only strengthens this judgment.

James, Paul and the Great Economic Crisis

Within a decade or so after Pentecost, the church in Jerusalem had become ravaged by persecution and poverty. The epistle of James and the writings of Paul both reflect this changed situation, and their responses, while sparse, must be considered here.

There is considerable opinion in scholarship that James (like Luke, it is believed) condemned the rich and favored disinvestment and poverty as the preferred spiritual condition.[21] It is true that James, more so than any New Testament author save perhaps Luke, places wealth at the structural center of his letter. But is it also true, as Barry Gordon writes, that "the writer of James gives the strongest impressions that this [disinvestment] is the only wise course for a Christian with assets"?[22]

Obviously written to exhort poor Christians, James indeed contains a profound critique of the rich. First, very like Jesus (his lilies of the field speech), he relativizes the importance of wealth. Riches are fleeting; they do not bring happiness, and so poverty is not the worst possible condition to be in (Jas 1:9-10). Like Jesus (his parable of the rich fool), James blasts those who think commerce and trade will bring them real security (Jas 4:13-17). The rich should "weep and wail" for the miseries that they will suffer (Jas 5:1-4). Like Jesus, James blessed the poor Christians, for God has chosen them—the "poor in the world"—to be "rich in faith and to be heirs of the kingdom" (Jas 2:5). Meanwhile, like the Prophets and Wisdom of old, he cites the rich for living evil economic lives. They have "dishonored the poor" and exploited Christians by dragging them into court (2:6).

Nevertheless, it is not immediately obvious that James's statements support the conclusions drawn by Gordon and many others. Placed in the context of the moral world of the Prophets and the Wisdom literature, a very different reading emerges. This one centers on the use of wealth, rather than on the evil of riches in themselves. Riches are evil on the conditions that people make them absolute ends of life, and especially when they become an altar on which to sacrifice the poor. Under such conditions, as Proverbs and Jesus promised, it is better to remain poor. Wisdom—yes; prophetic—yes. In keeping with the spirit of Jesus—yes, again. But none of this implies that James denies the possibility and goodness of riches in a context of faith and righteous action. James stands as a prophetic warning to the rich and thus as a powerful document of advocacy for the poor. It is a peculiar source of encouragement to the poor in their misery, if not a manifesto to social transformation.

The apostle Paul also wrote, albeit sparingly, on Christian economic life. The background for his teaching was mainly the disastrous situation of crisis in Jerusalem. During the peak years of his work as an apostle (from about A.D. 48 to 56), Paul worked intensely to collect money for "the poor among the saints at Jerusalem" (Rom 15:25-27).²³ He mentions this collection in several of his letters.²⁴ The most important reference is in 2 Corinthians 8 and 9. Because Paul's reasoning is complex, and because many writers oversimplify his argument, we must quote him at length. He begins, "For you know the generous act of our Lord Jesus Christ, that though he was rich, yet for your sakes he became poor, so that by his poverty you might become rich" (2 Cor 8:9).

Paul recommends a pattern of equality or fairness.

I do not mean that there should be relief for others and pressure on you, but it is a question of a *fair balance* between your present abundance and their need, so that their abundance may be for your need, in order that there may be a *fair balance*. As it is written, "The one who had much did not have too much, and the one who had little did not have too little." (2 Cor 8:13-15; italics mine)

He finishes his appeal with this explanation:

The point is this: the one who sows sparingly will also reap sparingly, and the one who sows bountifully will also reap bountifully. Each of you must give as you have made up your mind, not reluctantly or under compulsion, for God loves a cheerful giver. And God is able to provide you with every blessing in abundance, so that by always having enough of everything, you may share abundantly in every good work. As it is written, "He scatters abroad, he gives to the poor; his righteousness endures forever." He who supplies seed to the sower and bread for food will supply and multiply your seed for sowing and increase the harvest of your righteousness. You will be enriched in every way for your great generosity, which will produce thanksgiving to God through us. (2 Cor 9:6-11)

We must try to keep in view all of the elements of these passages, as well as the historical background, as we interpret them.

Understandably, modern theologians often cite these verses to support theologies of liberation through simpler living.[25] The norm, Sider suggests, is "economic equality among the people of God."[26] Paul's reference to Israel eating manna in the wilderness becomes the model for global economic fellowship. We should take to heart the example of "some greedy souls," who "apparently tried to gather more than they could use."[27] According to Sider, all excess ought to be spread around, so that there might be equality.[28] We are back to the manna of utilitarianism on a global-church scale.

However, beneath this reading and application is the unguarded assumption that Paul intended to establish general rules for Christian economic living—in all times and circumstances. But thorough recent studies suggest that this assumption may be false. Various scholars point out that Paul was not here collecting for world relief, or even for the world church. The collection was exclusively for the church in Jerusalem during its critical moment. Jouette Bassler, for instance, argues that Paul's main concern was not even the economic poverty of Christians in Jerusalem.[29] His main concern was rather with the connection between Israel and the church, with saving the relationship between the older covenant and the newer one, with promoting the salvation of his own people and with preserving the basic traditions needed for Christianity to be a system of faith and life that was at all meaningful. "This act of charity became for him a way of repairing the strained relationship between two wings of the church."[30]

So let us consider another interpretation of Paul's appeal to Christ's humiliation and to the story of the manna in the wilderness. For Paul, this special crisis was a matter of nearness. It was not suffering in the abstract that generated his moral appeal, but rather this particular poverty that was so very close to the heart of his life and mission as an apostle of Jesus Christ, first to the Jews, then to the Greeks. His was a theology that was boundaried by a deeply proximate moral crisis, not a paradigm for all of economic life.

This awareness helps to put his language of sacrifice and equality into perspective. As Luke Johnson judges, the great collection expressed a truth about the history of redemption. Jew and Christian were of the same root. Johnson thus writes:

> Although Paul is speaking the language of social leveling, it is clear that the equality he has in mind is the reciprocity of care, a dialectic of service: If the Gentiles have come to share in their spiritual blessings, they ought also to be of service to them in material blessings (Rom. 15:27).[31]

The reference to the manna and the powerful imagery of Christ's incarnation—that for our sakes "he became poor"—thus did not mean to "level off economic conditions." The purpose was, as Johnson puts it, "to stir his communities to an appropriate response to the needs of others."[32] Paul issues dramatic exhortations to love, in this special crisis, in the manner of Christ's sacrificial love, with faith that manna will appear every day. Thus, this text ought to guide us more in times of peculiar crisis than as a paradigm for all of economic life. Of course, by application, the crisis probably will not be the same for all Christians everywhere. The text leaves open the option, too, of an unusually selfless economic life—one thinks of Mother Teresa—but it does not mandate this, and again we must be wary of escapist, messianic tendencies in ourselves as we face the mundane work before us.[33]

Our reading is supported by the remaining sections of the passages we quoted earlier. The downward movements of Paul's appeal are qualified afterward by upward ones. As we have seen, he promises that God will provide bountifully. If we give, Paul writes, the Lord will "provide you with every blessing in abundance" (2 Cor 9:8). The end of sacrifice ("the one who sows bountifully") is not leveling, poverty or degradation, but that we may "reap bountifully." Obligation is not framed by images of crucifixion and death, ultimately, but by words of blessing and prosperity for further redemptive action. If we may apply this to ourselves, with respect to our own special, sacrificial responses to crisis, the Christ-drama is also about God's desire to keep us and to "increase [our] harvest" (2 Cor 9:10).

Moreover, like Luke in Acts, Paul respected human freedom. The last thing he wanted was a system of legalistic compulsion, such as is required by the manna of utilitarianism. In the texts cited, he insists on the importance of authenticity, genuineness, giving no more than really comes from the heart. Giving must be "cheerful," not merely a matter of duty. Indeed, Christian blessing brings with it a sense of duty. We feel a duty to represent Jesus Christ, especially in times of extraordinary need relevant to our circumstances. And the manna teaches us to have faith that God will supply us when we risk security for the right reasons. But we remember, faith in the wilderness was not an argument for paucity in perpetuity. As Paul suggests, a right sense of duty brings a spirit of freedom and abundance to everything. Faith in manna brought them into the land of "milk and honey." Thus he ends with images of abundance, not scarcity, with exhortations to multiply and be fruitful in the midst of labors. Paul's vision of their future was a model of servant-dominion not unlike what we found in the narratives and laws of the exodus. As servants (with all of the requisite qualifications from Job), the people would reign and prosper.

In sum, Paul responds to a special economic crisis with a most creative and powerful economic use of Christ's incarnation and life. Just as the God of the exodus used his might to liberate and empower Israel, so did his Son give of himself for our sake—that we might become rich. The appeal is not so much a principled negation of richness for all time as it is a response to an emergency. If Christians may for a time be deprived of their abundance, like Israel in the desert, the point and purpose holds fast to the vision of flourishing. Flourishing—in this world, or in the world to come? Paul does not elaborate, although his language is open to the worldly option. "You will be enriched in every way for your great generosity" (2 Cor 9:11). And of course the response, again, was voluntary, not even morally necessary: "Each of you must give as you have made up your mind, not reluctantly or under compulsion" (2 Cor 9:7).[34]

Unfinished Postscript:
To My Former Student (& Other Uneasy Rich Christians)

To my former student, whose story I told at the beginning of this book, I must now say what I did not have the words to say that day when he came to my office. You will remember that he had been on an urban program that sent him into a real crisis of economic identity. His conscience had overwhelmed him with guilt and self-hate, and indeed he is not alone in this. My message to him (and to my readers) now is that there is a gospel of liberation and affirmation for Christians with money. It is a gospel that weds the themes of royal dominion and delight and the compassion of the servant.

Of course much is wrong with American corporate culture. But I have come to believe that there is much that is good about its original principles and basic structures. I have learned late (because it was not taught in college when I was a student) that our institutions embody a vision of human liberty and happiness that resonates, more than I was led to think, with the vision of life that is revealed in the Scriptures. There is, I believe, plenty of room in our professional system to express a genuine Christian identity. Both systems—the biblical and the liberal democratic—are about making human beings larger and better at the same time. They honor the dignity of individuals, they express that dignity in terms both material and moral, and they demand a sense of corporate responsibility. If there is another cultural system that does so, I am unfamiliar with it.

Perhaps I am overreacting to those who disparage out of hand the reconciliation between Christianity and our culture. But overreaction cuts both ways. And I keep coming back to the metaphor of the royal man and woman. In very different ways, this metaphor emerges repeatedly in the sacred story. The best way I know to focus on the many questions about economic life is to ask, "What is my realm of dominion?" For me this question makes things clearer. If you imagine your vocation or calling as a kind of kingdom or realm, then maybe you will begin to see more clearly both your blessings and obligations. If God has called you to manufacture computer software, for instance, then you have a realm to think about. What is the nature of dominion, compassion and delight in that realm? What sorts of blessings and obligations come with such a gift and calling? But here is an important lesson. Scripture will not answer these personal questions for you. Nor will the church, and nor will I. After you have consulted with all the wisest and best authorities, and listened to their advice, you must eventually stand up and assume responsibility for your own life, as Paul writes, "with fear and trembling." That is the human condition, being made in the image and likeness of God, with the capacity and obligation to rule and to be fruitful and multiply, and fill the earth with good. God is not a spoonfeeder, and I suspect that that is what my student wanted him to be. Most of us do. But alas, God wants us to grow up: his moral universe is not Never Never Land; nor is it the realm of the Pied Piper. It was designed mainly for adults.

Prayer is basic too. And part of prayer (although evangelical Christians are often taught to reject it) is listening for the inner resonance and harmony with certain visions and possible directions, learning to know when we are being true to ourselves or when we are not, when we are "forcing it." Of course we have to listen to other people. The voices of our parents, teachers, friends, spouses, relatives and others speak through us all the time, and if we are lucky there is wisdom in what they say. And we have Scripture. This whole book is about the larger vision of creation, exodus, incarnation and community. In this the Word of God enlightens us all. But in the end, in a universe of individual souls, integrity must be somewhat different for everyone. As Paul put it, "Each of you must give as you have made up your mind" (2 Cor 9:7). Part of being royal is being given the responsibility to make decisions, to stand by them and to live manfully or womanfully with the consequences—one of which may be the disapproval of the crowds. (Jesus certainly understood this.)

One last thing. There also comes a time when "justification" (being declared "good" by God) means just that—God has declared *you*, yourself, your entire redeemed (even middle-class) identity as good. That is the end of the law of sin and death. That is the end of judgment. And that is the end of guilt over who you are. In this end is your beginning.

Notes

Chapter 1: The Identity Crisis of Rich Christians

[1]Ronald J. Sider, *Rich Christians in an Age of Hunger*, rev. ed. (Dallas: Word, 1990).

[2]See Justo Gonzalez, *Faith and Wealth* (San Francisco: Harper & Row, 1990), for a very useful survey of Christian perspectives on wealth among theologians in the church up to the fifth century. See also Barry Gordon, *The Economic Problem in Biblical and Patristic Thought* (Leiden, Netherlands: Brill, 1989).

Chapter 2: Christians & Money Through the Centuries

[1]Justo Gonzalez, *The Story of Christianity* (San Francisco: Harper & Row, 1984), p. xvii.

[2]See Gonzalez, *Faith and Wealth*, and also Barry Gordon, *The Economic Problem in Biblical and Patristic Thought* (Leiden, Netherlands: Brill, 1989). The reader should be advised that Gonzalez, while the more readable of the two, tends to view the early church as having a fairly unified answer, one that comports with his stress on community as in the book of Acts. Gordon is more sympathetic to the reconstructions of biblical criticism (especially "source criticism" and "tradition history") than many evangelical readers are likely to be, and his book is much more technical and difficult to read than is Gonzalez's. A strength of Gordon's presentation, though, is that it is sensitive to nuances, especially differences between early Christian thinkers, that are missed by Gonzalez. Also a strength, especially regarding early Christian thinking, is Gordon's attempt to explain things in their diverse social contexts throughout the Roman Empire.

[3]I am using the term *types* in the sense that H. R. Niebuhr used it in his famous book *Christ and Culture* (New York: Harper Torch Books, 1951), esp. pp. 39-40. He identifies five "typical answers" to the perennial question of Christ and culture. They range

from world-denial to world-accommodation. My "types" of Christian economic identity only loosely parallel his. I have chosen not to include a survey of the so-called Anabaptists, radical Protestants who took communalistic positions on Christian economic identity and life. Their positions are handled implicitly in the several sections where the mainline biblical warrant for personal property is presented, especially in chapter nine on the Jerusalem model in Acts.

[4]"Even in the year 1800, with a population of only four million inhabitants, the U.S. had given birth to more business corporations than the rest of the world combined." From *Toward the Future:* Catholic Social Thought and the U.S. Economy—A Lay Letter by the Lay Commission on Catholic Social Thinking, published by the American Catholic Committee (1984), p. 13.

[5]In the year 1884, the Catholic bishops of America wrote these words (intriguing for their contrast to the bishops' letter on the American system in 1985): "We consider the establishment of our country's independence, the shaping of its liberties and laws as a work of special Providence, its framers 'building wiser than they knew,' the Almighty's hand guiding them." Cited in ibid., p. vi.

[6]The word *gnostic* comes from the Greek word for "knowledge." So-called Gnostics claimed to have special, revealed knowledge that would enable their souls, or essential selves, to be liberated from the prisonhouse of the body and material existence. For a sympathetic and readable treatment of the subject, see Elaine Pagels, *The Gnostic Gospels* (New York: Random House, 1980).

[7]For a good survey of these centuries and Augustine's views on wealth, see Gonzalez, *Faith and Wealth*, pp. 214-22.

[8]For surveys of the changes brought about by the conversion of Constantine, see Justo Gonzalez, *The Story of Christianity* (San Francisco: Harper & Row, 1984), 1:112-35; for a more detailed look at the economic problem, see Gordon, *Economic Problem*, especially pp. 89-100. Gordon points out that, besides the prosperity, a larger pattern of stagnation and economic strangulation throughout the Empire encircled the church, so that monasticism might have been escape from either luxury *or* poverty, depending on the situation.

[9]The classic instance was Tertullian (160-c. 220); see Gonzalez, *Faith and Wealth*, 1:73-78.

[10]The classic counterpoint to Tertullian was Clement of Alexandria (150-215); see Gordon, *Economic Problem*, pp. 84-88. Clement appears to have been the sole voice among the church fathers for the potential good to be done through entrepreneurship and capital (ibid., p. 87 and notes).

[11]See ibid., pp. 101-4, for a list of such theologians and a discussion of John Chrysostom (344-407), one of the ablest speakers for communalism as a church and social model.

[12]See, for instance, Chrysostom's compromise, in ibid., pp. 109-10.

[13]See ibid., especially pp. 106-9. See also Gonzalez, *Faith and Wealth*, passim.

[14]The distinction between *having* things and *using* them as genuine "goods" goes back to earlier theologians such as Clement of Alexandria. See Gordon, *Economic Problem*, pp. 84-88.

¹⁵Some theologians distinguished between the validity of owning property as *land,* on the one hand, and owning other forms of property as gained through commercial efforts. St. Ambrose (339-397), for instance, affirmed the one but not the other. See ibid., p. 117. Augustine apparently broadened the scope of his basic affirmation to include both forms of ownership (p. 124). Also, some theologians had affirmed the goodness of property but only in its communal, rather than private, form (p. 113). Augustine, rather, affirmed personal property as both a natural and a divinely given right, subject though to moral conditions (p. 123).

¹⁶Augustine, *City of God,* abridged, ed. V. Bourke, trans. G. Walsh, Demetrius B. Zema, Grace Monahan and Daniel Honan (Garden City, N.Y.: Doubleday/Image Books, 1958), p. 255.

¹⁷Augustine *On Christian Doctrine* 1. 3. 9, trans. D. W. Robertson Jr. (New York: Liberal Arts Press, 1958). In eliminating Augustine's clause about that class of things meant to be both used *and* enjoyed, Gonzalez gives the impression that Augustine's classification was more rigid and simplistic than it actually was. See Gonzalez, *Faith and Wealth,* p. 215.

¹⁸Augustine *On Christian Doctrine* 1. 3. 9.

¹⁹Ibid.

²⁰Ibid.

²¹Ibid.

²²Ibid.

²³Ibid., 1. 4. 10. Perhaps our homeland is among things to be both enjoyed and used, but it is difficult to see the coherence in this proposal with Augustine's final claims.

²⁴*Sermones* 206. 4, in *Patrologiae Cursus Completus, Series Latina,* ed. J.-P. Migne (Paris: Garnier, 1834-).

²⁵*In Psalmos* 147. 12, in *Patrologiae Cursus Completus.*

²⁶*In Psalmos* 95. 15, in *Patrologiae Cursus Completus;* cited in Gonzalez, *Faith and Wealth,* pp. 215-16.

²⁷*Sermones* 85. 5, in *Patrologiae Cursus Completus,* and discussion by Gonzalez, *Faith and Wealth,* p. 219.

²⁸See again the discussion of the debate between separationists like Tertullian (160-?) and world-affirmative thinkers like Clement of Alexandria in Gordon, *Economic Problem,* pp. 81-88, and Niebuhr, *Christ and Culture.*

²⁹For a sound, readable discussion of monastic views on vocation, see Lee Hardy, *The Fabric of This World* (Grand Rapids, Mich.: Eerdmans, 1991).

³⁰The mainstream of Catholic thought stayed within the banks carved by Augustine. For example, Thomas Aquinas (1224-1274) wrote in brilliant detail to defend property as inherent in human dignity. Although he did not employ the words *use* and *enjoyment* in a rigid, contrasting manner, he did argue rigorously against "superfluous" wealth (with some concession to the difficulty of defining this exactly), and he made love of God and neighbor the keys to right use of one's goods. He also upheld the counsel of monasticism, and he maintained the traditional view that charging interest (usury) on loans was morally evil. For Thomas's views see especially *Summa Theologiae,* vol.

33, trans. W. J. Hill, and vol. 34, trans. R. J. Batten (New York: McGraw-Hill, 1963).

[31]Radical Protestants (sometimes called Anabaptists) challenged individual ownership in the sixteenth century; see, for instance, G. H. Williams, *The Radical Reformation*, 3rd ed. (Kirksville, Mo.: 16th Century Journal Publications, 1992). Below we shall encounter modern liberation theology, which has sometimes adopted communal property theory; several contemporary North American models, such as Ronald Sider, *Rich Christians in an Age of Hunger*, rev. ed. (Dallas: Word, 1990), while not explicitly communalistic, are very critical of individual claims of ownership in what have come to be standard Western Christian forms.

[32]The great social historian Max Weber originated this theory in his groundbreaking articles "The Protestant Sects and the Spirit of Capitalism." His thesis is discussed at length in *Protestantism and Capitalism: The Weber Thesis and Its Critics*, ed. Robert Green (Boston: Heath, 1959), p. vii. See references in the text below to discussions of its validity.

[33]See Hardy, *Fabric of This World*, pp. 44-77.

[34]On this see Luther's essay "An Appeal to the Ruling Class," in *Martin Luther*, ed. and trans. John Dillenberger (Garden City, N.Y.: Doubleday/Anchor Books, 1961).

[35]See also his comments on food and drink in ibid., p. 483.

[36]John Calvin, *Institutes of the Christian Religion*, ed. John T. McNeill, trans. Ford Lewis Battles, Library of Christian Classics 20 (Philadelphia: Westminster Press, 1967), p. 841 (3. 19). Note that Calvin's qualification of acquiring goods—by inheritance and cultivation thereof—preserved a longstanding Christian bias toward that kind of acquisition, and it leaves other kinds in doubt.

[37]Ibid., p. 689 (3. 7).

[38]Ibid., p. 692.

[39]Ibid., p. 695.

[40]Ibid., p. 841 (3. 19).

[41]For a good discussion of this process, see *Toward the Future*.

[42]See ibid., p. 23.

[43]John T. McNeill, *The History and Character of Calvinism* (New York: Oxford University Press, 1954), p. 419.

[44]Cited in *Toward the Future*, p. 23.

[45]Ibid., p. 13.

[46]As early as 1738, commenting on the Lord's blessing to Israel in Deuteronomy 15:7-12, the great Puritan preacher Jonathan Edwards wrote words that I do not believe Augustine, Aquinas, Luther or Calvin could have written in their times: "But if you place your happiness in God, in glorifying Him and serving him by doing good, in this way above all others you will promote your wealth and honor and pleasure here below, and obtain hereafter a crown of unfading glory and pleasures forevermore at God's right hand" (*Charity and Its Fruits* [1738], quoted in McNeill, *History and Character of Calvinism*, p. 342).

[47]See, for instance, the severe cultural criticism of Christopher Lasch, *The Culture of Narcissism* (New York: Warner Books, 1979), especially pp. 105-16, and Tom Sine, *The*

Mustard Seed Conspiracy (Waco, Tex.: Word, 1981), especially pp. 45-52.

[48]Zig Ziglar, assuring his readers that faith in Christ gives assurance of material wealth, punctuated his remarks by accusing anyone who might think otherwise of "stinkin' thinkin'." Cited in Sine, *Mustard Seed*, p. 79.

[49]Television broadcast in the winter of 1992. One intriguing version of this model names itself "reconstructionism." It has developed and gained enough of a following in this country to be featured on a Bill Moyers special for public television. Reconstructionists seek to "reconstruct" a biblical society on the literal lines of Old Testament law. The assumption is that a nation based on such principles would be righteous, and would thus prosper immensely, while other alternatives (such as socialism or secular capitalism) will necessarily lead to ruin, since they violate the created moral order.

[50]A very useful introduction to liberation theology in its diverse forms is *The Future of Liberation Theology: Essays in Honor of Gustavo Gutiérrez*, ed. M. Ellis and O. Maduro (Maryknoll, N.Y.: Orbis, 1989).

[51]For example, see the strongly presented work by black theologian James Cone, *God of the Oppressed* (New York: Seabury Press, 1981). See also the book of essays referred to in the previous note.

[52]An unexpected version of this thesis among prominent Reformed thinkers is that of Nicholas Wolterstorff, *Until Justice and Peace Embrace* (Grand Rapids, Mich.: Eerdmans, 1983), especially pp. 73-98. An important popular American version of the rising utilitarian view is Ron Sider's *Rich Christians in an Age of Hunger*. He urges rich Christians to consider alternative vocations and "simpler" lifestyles. He exhorts Christians to live lives that express "identification" with the poor. Indeed, a dominant theme in much Christian literature today is opposed to the bourgeois spirit of industry and acquisitiveness. It is said that "less is better," or that "small is beautiful." See E. F. Schumacher, *Small Is Beautiful: Economics As If People Mattered* (New York: Harper & Row, 1973). While these writers are not liberation theologians in the usual sense of that term (for one thing, they disavow communism), they do identify God's cause with the poor in a manner that leaves little place for affirmation of the rich or lives of superfluous "delight." Wolterstorff does seek to affirm "delight," but does not appear to have quite the needed categories for doing so unambiguously.

[53]The popular evangelical theology seems not very well grounded in the theory and practice of charity that was stressed by early American Christians. Liberation theology seems not very well grounded in the historic Christian assertion of property as the expression of individual human dignity and as the anchor of true justice in societies. On this last point, there is a growing school of serious Christian thought that points out this problem very forcefully. One of the leading figures is Catholic writer Michael Novak; see his *The Spirit of Democratic Capitalism* (Lanham, Md.: University Press of America/Madison Books, 1991); see also Brian Griffiths, *The Creation of Wealth* (Downers Grove, Ill.: InterVarsity Press, 1985), and Richard John Neuhaus, *Doing Well and Doing Good* (New York: Doubleday, 1992). On a popular and practical level, see Rich DeVos, *Compassionate Capitalism: People Helping People Help Themselves* (New York: Dutton, 1993).

Chapter 3: We Live in a Material World

[1]George Landes makes this point very forcefully in his scholarly but readable essay "Creation and Liberation," in *Creation in the Old Testament*, ed. B. Anderson (Philadelphia: Fortress, 1984), pp. 135-51. Ron Sider's widely read book *Rich Christians in an Age of Hunger*, rev. ed. (Dallas: Word, 1990), suffers greatly from this typical lack of attention to the primary themes of creation, especially those of what I later call "dominion and delight." The same criticism, in somewhat different form, applies to Barry Gordon, *The Economic Problem in Biblical and Patristic Thought* (Leiden, Netherlands: Brill, 1989). His focus on the "Yahwistic" source, or "J" (roughly Gen 2—3), excludes from view the essential cosmic vision of Genesis 1 and its largely affirmative vision of the world. Perhaps that is why his account centers first on the Fall in relation to work and fails to notice the powerful theme of abundance and delight that threads through the whole creation narrative. Also (as Landes shows), this is generally true of liberation theology, causing a subordination of creation to the theme of redemption. Just how grave this error is will emerge clearly at many points in this book.

[2]For a good study of this intriguing subject by a committed Christian scholar, see *The Babylonian Genesis*, trans. and ed. Alexander Heidel, 2nd ed. (Chicago: University of Chicago Press, 1963). *Enuma Elish* is one of several ancient creation stories that help us to interpret Genesis 1—3 in their cultural context. Heidel also points out interesting similarities between Genesis and the myths. But the most remarkable thing is the differences.

[3]See, for example, the widely influential book by Robert Bellah et al., *Habits of the Heart* (Berkeley: University of California Press, 1985). This is a most provocative, if not very cheerful, essay on the present state of the American character.

[4]See the brilliant work by Henri Frankfort, *The Intellectual Adventure of Ancient Man* (Chicago: University of Chicago Press, 1977).

[5]Frankfort wrote of the Egyptians: "The sky might be thought of as a material vault above the earth, or as a cow, or as a female. A tree might be a tree or a female who was the tree-goddess. . . . A god might be depicted as a man, or as a falcon, or as a falcon-headed man. . . . There was thus a continuing substance across the phenomena of the universe. . . . The universe is a spectrum in which one color blends off into another without line of demarcation" (ibid., p. 62).

[6]See, for example, the classic essay by Lynn White Jr., "The Historical Roots of Our Ecological Crisis," in *Science*, March 10, 1967, pp. 12-26. His idea popularized the theory of the great historian Arnold Toynbee; see James Nash, *Loving Nature* (Nashville: Abingdon, 1991). I shall return to it below.

[7]Nash writes that White's thesis has become almost synonymous with contemporary "Earth Day" ideology; see Nash, *Loving Nature*, p. 69.

[8]See Heidel, *Babylonian Genesis*, especially pp. 118-26, and Frankfort, *Intellectual Adventure*, p. 182.

[9]See the survey of this doctrine in C. Braaten and R. Jenson, *Christian Dogmatics* (Philadelphia: Fortress, 1984), 1:330-33. Also K. Barth, *Church Dogmatics*, 3/1, ed. G. W. Bromiley and T. F. Torrance (Edinburgh: T. & T. Clark, 1957), pp. 192-206. Some

traditions have focused on the intellect, others on morality, others on spirituality, others on relationality and personhood, still others on creativity and freedom. Barth judges that the dominant theory in a given time usually says more about the time and culture than about the meaning of the language of Genesis.

[10]See Frankfort, *Intellectual Adventure*.

[11]Here I am mainly dependent on an essay by David Clines, "A Biblical Doctrine of Man," from an unpublished syllabus used at Fuller Theological Seminary in 1972. I do not know whether this useful material has since been published. See also the similar commentary of Gerhard von Rad, *Genesis* (Philadelphia: Westminster Press, 1972), p. 58.

[12]Ibid., p. 60.

[13]The Hebrew word translated "subdue" is a very strong one. Writes von Rad: "The expressions for the exercise of dominion are remarkably strong: *rada*, 'tread,' 'trample' (e.g., the wine press); similarly *kabas*, 'stamp' " (ibid., p. 60).

[14]I refer again to what has now come to be called "the Lynn White thesis." So Nash, *Loving Nature*.

[15]Classical Christian theology such as H. Bavinck, *The Doctrine of God*, trans. William Hendriksen (1951; reprint Grand Rapids, Mich.: Baker Book House, 1979), presents God's power mainly in the context of God's abstract omnipotence. A modern exception is the work by Emil Brunner, *The Christian Doctrine of God*, trans. Olive Wyon (Philadelphia: Westminster Press, 1949). Also Karl Barth, *Church Dogmatics*, 2/1, ed. G. W. Bromiley and T. F. Torrance (Edinburgh: T. & T. Clark, 1957). These works bring together the omnipotence and the love of God, with focus on the work of Jesus Christ as the supreme expression of God's power.

[16]A careful reading of Genesis 1 reminds us that the man and woman were both made in God's image and to both he gave dominion. In the second creation narrative of Genesis 2—3, in spite of traditional readings, the text makes clear that the man and the woman are coequal partners in life, each committed to the well-being of the other. For an extended discussion of male and female in Genesis 2—3, see Phyllis Trible, *God and the Rhetoric of Sexuality* (Philadelphia: Fortress, 1978).

[17]The issue of "rule over" comes to a head in the biblical narratives on the establishment of monarchy in Israel. God warns against this system as unnatural and open to abuse. See John Bright, *The Kingdom of God* (Nashville: Abingdon, 1953), pp. 32-33.

[18]For a thoroughly rigorous and challenging study of the body in the Old Testament, see John Cooper, *Body, Soul and Life Everlasting* (Grand Rapids, Mich.: Eerdmans, 1989).

[19]See Karl Barth, *Church Dogmatics*, 3/2, ed. G. W. Bromiley and T. F. Torrance (Edinburgh: T. & T. Clark, 1958), pp. 325-436. Citation p. 351.

[20]Not coincidentally, the prophets and Jesus envisioned the kingdom of God in images of a royal banquet and never-ending feast, as we shall see.

[21]*King Lear*, act 2, scene 4.

[22]William James, *The Will to Believe*, cited in Robert Bly, *Iron John* (New York: Vintage Books, 1990), pp. 224-25.

[23]On Jefferson's view of Scripture and the material world, see Daniel Boorstin, *The Lost World of Thomas Jefferson* (1948; reprint Chicago: University of Chicago Press, 1981), especially "Jeffersonian Christianity," pp. 151-66.

[24]See the scholarly article by Malcolm Clark, "The Legal Background to the Yahwist's Use of 'Good and Evil' in Genesis 2—3," *Journal of Biblical Theology* 88 (September 1969): 266-78. "The Yahwist" refers to a scholarly consensus that Genesis 2—3 was once a second creation account, originally distinct from that of Genesis 1.

[25]See H. Richard Niebuhr, *Christ and Culture* (New York: Harper & Row/Harper Torch Books, 1951).

[26]My assumption here is that not all economic systems or their ways of life are morally equal, but that they all express the goodness of creation and the badness of the Fall in varying degrees and proportions. The Christian must thus seek to discriminate between good and evil in any system; but it matters whether we look first for the evil or for the good.

Chapter 4: Liberty, Luxury & Liberation in the Exodus

[1]If the reader is interested in a scholarly survey of the composition and formation of the book of Exodus that is fairly comprehensible to the nonexpert, I recommend Brevard Childs, *Introduction to the Old Testament as Scripture* (Philadelphia: Fortress, 1982), pp. 161-79, 184.

[2]See N. K. Gottwald, "The Exodus as Event and Process: A Test Case in the Biblical Grounding of Liberation Theology," in *The Future of Liberation Theology*, ed. M. Ellis and O. Maduro (Maryknoll, N.Y.: Orbis, 1989), pp. 250-60.

[3]Ronald J. Sider, *Rich Christians in an Age of Hunger*, rev. ed. (Dallas: Word, 1990), p. 41. Here Sider acknowledges that economic liberation was not the *only* concern, but insists that it was at the core of God's concerns in redeeming his people. Gustavo Gutiérrez expresses the opinion that characterizes the movement: "The liberation of Israel is a political action. It is the breaking away from a situation of despoliation and misery and the beginning of a just and comradely society" (*A Theology of Liberation: History, Politics and Salvation*, trans. and ed. Caridad Inda and John Eagleson [Maryknoll, N.Y.: Orbis, 1973], p. 155).

[4]On "structural evil" and the nature of "social justice" in the Old Testament, see Stephen Mott, *Biblical Ethics and Social Change* (New York: Oxford University Press, 1982), p. 59, for a very good summary.

[5]See Lawrence Adams, "Christianity and Economics: New Documents for the 90's," *Religion and Economics Quarterly*, Summer 1990. This is a very good summary of the differences between members of the World Council of Churches on the one side and representatives of the Oxford Conference on the other. The one group tends to envision the just society as highly controlled by government measures for redistributing wealth. The other focuses more on freedom and property rights as means of liberating the poor.

[6]On the connection, see the very readable book by James Limburg, *The Prophets and the Powerless* (Atlanta: John Knox Press, 1977).

[7]Its name is derived from its repeated words: "You shall be holy, for I the LORD your God am holy." The teachings of the Holiness Code gave Israel a summary and definition of holiness. They are thus of utmost importance to a biblical vision of life. For a detailed discussion of the Holiness Code and its literary history, see Childs, *Old Testament*, pp. 182-89.

[8]This is the basis for the historic Christian condemnation of charging interest as immoral (usury). More recent Christians (siding with Jewish tradition) have pointed out that the text forbids charging interest to a poor brother. It is not a blanket prohibition.

[9]For a discussion of the relationship between Leviticus and Deuteronomy in Israel's history, see Barry Gordon, *The Economic Problem in Biblical and Patristic Thought* (Leiden, Netherlands: Brill, 1989), pp. 11-20. The approaches to economic life in these two are essentially alike in principle, but in Leviticus, which was later than Deuteronomy, some scholars detect what Gordon describes as "new vistas." These are "fresh insights concerning the possibilities of economic growth; a new universalism (concern for life beyond the culture) and a renewed probing of the meaning of work" (p. 15). These observations, especially the first one, are pertinent to some of my later points about the sympathy of Leviticus to productivity, growth and delight for all people.

[10]John Gladwin of the Church of England's Board for Social Responsibility writes of the jubilee: "God saw a need for a redistributive principle whose aim was to restore justice and peace. . . . The operations of the free market in land sales and its impact on people are not trusted in Scripture" ("Centralist Economics," in *Wealth and Poverty: Four Christian Views*, ed. Robert Clouse [Downers Grove, Ill.: InterVarsity Press, 1984], pp. 185-86).

[11]David Chilton writes that "the Jubilee was *typological:* that is, it was a symbolic prefiguring of the work of Jesus Christ." By this he means that its application today is only symbolic and it contains no significance for real economic life. See his *Productive Christians in an Age of Guilt Manipulators* (Tyler, Tex.: Institute for Christian Economics, 1981), pp. 156-57 and the whole chapter on the jubilee.

[12]The context of the laws is a pervasive concern for the poor as an expression of true godliness, and the jubilee (whether or not it was ever practiced) functions throughout Scripture to make this point emphatically to God's people. Thus Isaiah used the jubilee to help us imagine the coming kingdom of God (Is 61). The "jubilee kingdom" was a realm of freedom from oppression of every kind, including material poverty. The coming of the kingdom would be the "day of release" for the captives of the earth, a day of liberation and joy to the whole world in the most comprehensive manner imaginable. In Luke's Gospel, Jesus used the jubilee as the metaphor for his entire mission as the Messiah of God, the Holy One of Israel who would come to "proclaim release to the captives" (Lk 4:18). As we shall see (chapter six), this was indeed a "spiritual" jubilee, but not only that. The liberation of Jesus Christ also contains a powerful social message that is indeed good news to the economically and physically poor (Lk 4:18-19). The physical liberation of the captives becomes a glass

through which we begin to see the fullness of God's plan in Jesus Christ to bring about a kingdom of justice and peace. Here we see the metamorphosis of the jubilee as "law," its constancy as "value."

[13]Gordon observes that the law seems to favor agrarian pursuits in economic life. See examples in his *Economic Problem*, p. 19. He speculates that the reason for this was that rural people were more vulnerable to abuses in the credit system than were businesspeople in the towns and cities. This may have been true, but his explanation ignores the religious vision of the land as sacred and as a trust from God to his people that could not be violated.

[14]Sider, *Rich Christians*, p. 66; he writes further, "As absolute owner, God places limitations on the acquisition and use of property. According to the Old Testament, 'the right to property was clearly *subordinated* to the obligation to care for the weaker members of society.' That is the clear implication of the legislation on the jubilee, the sabbatical year, gleaning and interest" (p. 88). The quote within the citation is from New Testament scholar Martin Hengel, *Property and Riches in the Early Church*, trans. John Bowden (Ann Arbor, Mich.: University Microfilms/Books on Demand, n.d.), p. 12. See also *Through the Eye of the Needle*, published by the Department of Business and Economics at Calvin College in 1986 (1989), which states that "stewardship" is the main principle in Scripture for shaping a sound economic life. Because stewardship is defined in terms of weakened property rights, the consequence is inevitably a mostly critical disposition toward the free pursuit and possession of property.

[15]See Sider, *Rich Christians*, p. 135, for his specific application of the jubilee to the redistribution of our "pool of resources." Sider never explains how nations might follow suit without granting dictatorial powers to governments over corporations and individuals.

[16]For an extended discussion of the economics of this, see the commentary by Baruch A. Levine, *Leviticus*, JPS Torah Commentary (Philadelphia: Jewish Publication Society, 1989), especially p. 474. See also the somewhat more accessible (to laypersons) commentary by John Hartley, *Leviticus*, Word Bible Commentary (Dallas: Word, 1992), especially p. 415.

[17]Gutiérrez, *Theology of Liberation*, p. 295.

[18]Robert North, *The Sociology of the Biblical Jubilee* (Rome: Pontifical Biblical Institute, 1954), p. 163. This is a massive, technical and very insightful study of the subject. Notice also Gordon's cautious, independent agreement with the point North makes here. He rightly understands that the law, while it constrained abuses, did so in a manner that "helped structure the economy so that certain types of growth were more likely to occur than others" (*Economic Problem*, p. 19).

[19]North, *Sociology of the Biblical Jubilee*, p. 163.

[20]I owe the term "religious space" to Geoffrey R. Lilburne in his book *A Sense of Place: A Christian Theology of the Land* (Nashville: Abingdon, 1989), especially pp. 45-54 on the Hebrews and the land.

[21]On the jubilee as an institutional exodus, see R. Hubbard, "The Go'el in Ancient

Israel: Theological Reflections on an Israelite Institution," *Bulletin for Biblical Research* 1 (1991): 3-19.

[22]North, *Sociology of the Biblical Jubilee*, p. 218.

[23]North cites Karl Bahr, who makes this complex point very well: "On the one hand the people in relation to Yahweh were maintained in constant consciousness of their servitude, so that we find in no other people such a deep humbling beneath God's powerful hand; on the other hand in relation to men and other nations the feeling of freedom was strengthened by the jubilee" (quoted in ibid., p. 218, n. 3).

[24]Hartley, *Leviticus,* pp. 447-48.

[25]Sider, *Rich Christians,* p. 69.

[26]I see no reason to take the teachings of Deuteronomy 14:22-29 as inconsistent with those of Numbers 18:21-32. There is thus no need to explore the issue of historical development in Israel's law, which is generally beyond the scope of this book.

Chapter 5: The Prophets & Wisdom

[1]For a very good treatment of demonic evil and the social order in Scripture, see Stephen Mott, *Biblical Ethics and Social Change* (New York: Oxford University Press, 1982), pp. 6-10.

[2]See James Limburg, *The Prophets and the Powerless* (Atlanta: John Knox Press, 1977), p. 55. The preaching of Amos seems to have begun around 760 B.C. and seems primarily aimed at the Northern Kingdom; see Brevard Childs, *Introduction to the Old Testament as Scripture* (Philadelphia: Fortress, 1979), pp. 400-401, on this and other historical matters.

[3]Limburg, *Prophets,* p. 55.

[4]See ibid. On the more or less unified message of all of the prophets on wealth, see J. Barton Payne, *The Theology of the Older Testament* (Grand Rapids, Mich.: Zondervan, 1962), pp. 247-49.

[5]Limburg, *Prophets,* p. 62.

[6]Ronald J. Sider, *Rich Christians in an Age of Hunger,* rev. ed. (Dallas: Word, 1990), p. 56.

[7]See Mott, *Biblical Ethics,* pp. 59-63, on the terms *righteousness* and *justice.*

[8]For the main body of this section on Proverbs I am indebted to a paper by Raymond C. Van Leeuwen, "Wealth and Poverty: System and Contradiction in Proverbs," presented at the Religion and Theology Department Colloquium at Calvin College and at the Society of Biblical Literature in 1990. See also Raymond C. Van Leeuwen, "Enjoying Creation—Within Limits," in *The Midas Trap,* ed. David Neff (Wheaton, Ill.: Scripture Press/Victor Books, 1990), pp. 23-40.

[9]Ibid., p. 37.

[10]Ibid.

Chapter 6: The Social & Economic Standing of Jesus

[1]See Nicholas Wolterstorff, *When Justice and Peace Embrace* (Grand Rapids, Mich.: Eerdmans, 1983). Given my own upbringing, I can only read his self-description with great

sympathy: "I have learned of the radical origins of the tradition in which I was reared. Learning of those origins has given me a deepened appreciation of my own identity. It has also produced in me a profound discontent over my tradition's loss of its radicalism" (p. ix).

[2]See H. Richard Niebuhr, *Christ and Culture* (New York: Harper & Row/Harper Torch Books, 1951), pp. 11-29, for a classic treatment of Christ as deeply subversive to the structures of his own culture specifically and of culture generally.

[3]Compare Justo Gonzalez, *Faith and Wealth* (San Francisco: Harper & Row, 1990), pp. 72-75. All the works referred to in this section generally agree on this picture of the economic setting, with some differences.

[4]See Richard Horsely, *Jesus and the Spiral of Violence* (San Francisco: Harper & Row, 1987).

[5]W. Pilgrim, *Good News to the Poor* (Minneapolis: Augsburg, 1981), p. 45.

[6]Ibid.

[7]Ibid., p. 43.

[8]Ibid.

[9]Gonzalez, *Faith and Wealth*, p. 73.

[10]Richard Horsely with J. S. Hanson, *Bandits, Prophets and Messiahs: Popular Movements at the Time of Jesus* (San Francisco: Harper & Row, 1985), pp. 31-34.

[11]Ibid.

[12]Horsely, *Spiral of Violence*, p. 212.

[13]See John Stambaugh and David Balch, *The Social World of the First Christians* (London: SPCK, 1986), p. 77.

[14]Horsely contends that the tax collectors mentioned in the New Testament came mainly from this category. See *Spiral of Violence*, p. 212.

[15]See the remarkable encounter between a group of tax collectors and John the Baptist in Luke 3:12-15. The rigorist John makes what seems a very modest demand on them: "Don't collect any more than you are required to." See also ibid., pp. 213-14.

[16]It is so astonishing that it seems impossible to square with the image of the "radical Christ" as many understand him. This assumption, rather than the textual evidence, seems to have determined Horsely's conclusion that this aspect of the biblical witness must be untrue. See ibid., pp. 212-17. Horsely's conviction that Jesus would not have dealt sympathetically with "collaborators" seems to me to outweigh the arguments that he produces in its defense. It certainly outweighs his trust in this important aspect of the Gospel narrative and church tradition connected with it, and this of course speaks volumes about the *biblical* foundations for his interpretation of Jesus as the founder of a sort of counterinsurgency force in the Empire. For a thorough critique of the main sociological approaches to the Gospels, see B. Holmberg, *Sociology and the New Testament: An Appraisal* (Minneapolis: Augsburg/Fortress, 1990). Also, Thomas E. Schmidt, *Hostility to Wealth in the Synoptic Gospels* (Sheffield, U.K.: JSOT Press, 1987).

[17]S. Safrai, M. Stern, D. Flusser and W. C. van Unnink, eds., *The Jewish People in the First Century: Historical Geography, Political History, Social, Cultural and Religious Life and Institutions*, vol. 2 (Philadelphia: Fortress, 1987). See especially the informative essay

by S. Applebaum, "The Social and Economic Status of the Jews in the Diaspora," pp. 662-65.

[18]Ibid.

[19]Ibid.

[20]Ibid.

[21]It has been suggested that Jesus worked as a "builder" *(tektōn)* in stone and masonry rather than as a carpenter in woodworking. The reason for this is that most building in that region was done in brick, adobe and stone, for wood was expensive and in short supply by comparison. However, see Douglas Oakman, *Jesus and the Economic Question of His Day* (Lewiston, N.Y.: Edwin Mellen, 1986), pp. 176-82. Oakman shows that carpenters *(tektones)* normally worked in wood but that the craft made one a "jack of all trades." He is open to the position that the village of Nazareth specialized in carpentry.

[22]Applebaum, "Social and Economic Status."

[23]Ronald J. Sider, *Rich Christians in an Age of Hunger,* rev. ed. (Dallas: Word, 1990), p. 61.

[24]Ibid.

[25]For a thorough treatment of Jesus' vocation see John Paul II, *Laborem Exercens: On Human Work* (Sydney, Australia: St. Paul Publishers, 1981), pp. 99, 101. See also references in Barry Gordon, *The Economic Problem in Biblical and Patristic Thought* (Leiden, Netherlands: Brill, 1989), p. 47; and, again, Oakman, *Jesus and the Economic Question,* pp. 176-82.

[26]Pilgrim, *Good News,* p. 46. We see no a priori reason to doubt the tradition that Jesus worked at this particular trade.

[27]Martin Hengel, *Property and Riches in the Early Church,* trans. John Bowden (Ann Arbor, Mich.: University Microfilms/Books on Demand, n.d.), pp. 26-27. Later traditions (striking for their mundaneness in a context where Christ was worshiped as divine) say that he "made yokes and ploughs." On this see the reference to Justin Martyr. There are also reports that Jesus' grandnephews worked a small piece of land toward the end of the first century.

[28]Gordon writes, "The designation of Christ as 'a carpenter' is important in both theological and sociological terms. It indicates, amongst other things, that Jesus did not own a part of the Land, and that he was not amongst the poorest of the poor" *(Economic Problem,* p. 47). Gordon, however, does think that "this detail is of marginal relevance only for the evangelists' treatments of Jesus as a worker." Their focus is of course on his "work" during his public mission.

[29]See the book by Richard A. Batey, *Jesus and the Forgotten City* (Grand Rapids, Mich.: Baker Book House, 1992). Batey has challenged the standard wisdom that Jesus lived a poor, countrified existence. He gives evidence for thinking that southern Galilee was a much more cosmopolitan and sophisticated environment than is usually thought. And his research suggests that building in the region was much more architecturally complex and lucrative than is commonly believed. According to Batey, it is unthinkable that Jesus, living a mere two miles away, was not deeply involved in

the commercial system of that city's redevelopment. Batey's views are indirectly supported by the work of John Stambaugh and David Balch, *The Social World of the First Christians* (London: SPCK, 1986), especially pp. 92-94., on revising our picture of the status of southern Galilee. The research of Douglas Oakman leads strongly to the same conclusion; see *Jesus and the Economic Question*, pp. 180-82.

[30]See Stambaugh and Balch, *Social World*, p. 90.

[31]Compare Batey, *Jesus and the Forgotten City*, and references in previous note.

[32]So Stambaugh and Balch, *Social World*, p. 93.

[33]Douglas Oakman shows, however, that carpentry in Nazareth would necessarily be bound up with agrarian work. See *Jesus and the Economic Question*, p. 178.

[34]Sider, *Rich Christians*, p. 120.

[35]Ibid., p. 122.

[36]For a more extended critique of the contradictions within strategies of separatism, see Niebuhr, *Christ and Culture*.

[37]For a good discussion of the political dimension of Christ's work, see Richard Mouw, *Political Evangelism* (Grand Rapids, Mich.: Eerdmans, 1973); also John Howard Yoder, *The Politics of Jesus* (Grand Rapids, Mich.: Eerdmans, 1972). Twenty years later, both of these books retain their strong value.

[38]Most recent commentators reject the proposition that Jesus envisioned a "spiritual" jubilee only. The context in Isaiah, its own allusion to Leviticus 25 and the images of *physical* liberation that follow for the blind, lame, deaf and speechless all weigh against this view. See Pilgrim, *Good News*.

[39]This text is clearly a reference to Isaiah 35, in which the prophet envisions the messianic age as a time when the blind, lame, deaf and speechless will be released from their oppressions. Notably, Isaiah does not include the *poor* among those special beneficiaries of the coming kingdom. In Luke, significantly, Jesus has added this group to the list.

[40]Critics of Christianity have often used this claim as part of their attack against the faith. In the second century, Celsus despised Christianity because it made sense only to "the foolish, dishonorable and stupid, and only slaves, women, and little children." Celsus was convinced that Christianity had *always* been a movement among the lower classes, because Jesus had won his converts from the dregs of society, "tax collectors and sailors." Cited in Wayne Meeks, *The First Urban Christians: The Social World of the Apostle Paul* (New Haven, Conn.: Yale University Press, 1983), p. 51. In more modern times, philosophers such as Friedrich Nietzsche have seen this phenomenon as essential to the nature of Christianity itself. Nietzsche scorned Christianity for elevating the "pariah of society" to the top of the world order and for emasculating the truly great and powerful, dropping them to the bottom of the moral scale. The great historian Edward Gibbon blamed the antielitism of Christianity for the eventual collapse of the Roman Empire. In nuanced contrast, see Oakman, *Jesus and the Economic Question*, pp. 182-93, for a superb discussion of Jesus' social contacts.

[41]See Meeks, *First Urban Christians*, on the social origins of the churches founded by the apostle Paul.

[42]Ibid., p. 51.
[43]Ibid., p. 73.
[44]Ibid.
[45]Ibid.
[46]On this distinction of groups, see the useful discussion in G. Theissen, *Sociology of Early Palestinian Christianity* (Philadelphia: Fortress, 1977).
[47]Hengel, *Property and Riches*, p. 27.

Chapter 7: The Christ of Radical Compassion & Delight

[1]Catholic theology thus views such poverty as an optional ideal for special "saints." Protestants (especially Reform-minded ones) have stressed that Jesus' poverty is not to be imitated, but is a model of Christian sacrifice and self-denial. In recent years, liberation theologians claim that Jesus' poverty was a literal identification with the poor. In spite of these differences of interpretation, most Christians believe that Jesus called his followers to lives of poverty.

[2]Luke Johnson writes: "The problem is that the directives seem to be saying different things: they seem to point us in different directions." He warns against tendencies in theology, on various sides of issues, to harmonize the Gospels in one way or another. The outcome is selective interpretation. See Luke T. Johnson, *Sharing Possessions: Mandate and Symbol of Faith* (Philadelphia: Fortress, 1981), p. 12. So also Barry Gordon, *The Economic Problem in Biblical and Patristic Thought* (Leiden, Netherlands: Brill, 1989), who judges finally that Luke himself "failed to resolve the tensions he experienced concerning discipleship and the economic problem" (p. 70).

[3]I respect Johnson's resistance to "harmonization," but either we have two different people or we have just one very interesting and complex one. I choose to believe that the second is the more likely outcome, and will seek to show that in this chapter. See Johnson, *Sharing Possessions*, p. 12. The same response holds to Gordon, *Economic Problem*. I believe that both writers fail to see Luke's progress from an apparent and (for rich people) saliently terrifying model of disinvestment to something more in line with the exodus vision of the "righteous rich."

[4]Thomas E. Schmidt is quite correct to say of this imagery that "well-meaning attempts to shrink the camel (by the claim that Jesus said 'cable' rather than 'camel') or enlarge the needle (by the Medieval legend that there was a small gate in the wall of ancient Jerusalem called 'the needle's eye') are creative, but desperate." See his article "The Hard Sayings of Jesus," in *The Midas Trap*, ed. David Neff (Wheaton, Ill.: Scripture Press/Victor Books, 1990), p. 18. This weighs heavily against the Catholic tradition that makes the hard sayings into "counsels" for the special saints rather than "commands" for every Christian.

[5]Many commentators have observed that Luke writes "poor," rather than "poor in spirit," as Matthew puts it. This is consonant with Luke's stress on the interface between spiritual and economic life. However, as arguments below indicate, I do not believe that his meaning is very different from Matthew's. First of all, the "poor" addressed here are not the multitudes, but Jesus' inner circle of disciples. The "pov-

erty" that Jesus blesses must therefore be defined in terms of *theirs*. And careful reading shows that theirs was a messianic, or theological and spiritual, poverty more than it was literal and economic. The difference is that Luke stresses that spiritual lowliness must come to economic expression—but not that economic oppression entails spiritual lowliness and thus blessedness.

[6]There are many arguments against this view. I pass over the argument that the demand to surrender possessions, strictly speaking, is impossible to fulfill short of suicide. Thus Jesus would have given a command that not even he could have kept during his life. I also merely mention here that during his first thirty years he would have lived in blatant violation of his own condition for salvation. Furthermore, we shall see that certain texts in the Gospels portray him violating that condition even during his public mission. I will elaborate on this last point through the next section of this chapter.

[7]This was the bone in Gnosticism that the ancient church could not swallow. It would be interesting to see how Thomas E. Schmidt would distinguish his own position from that of the Gnostics sufficiently to avoid this shattering implication and the consequences discussed below. See Schmidt, "Hard Sayings of Jesus." Also see his book *Hostility to Wealth in the Synoptic Gospels* (Sheffield, U.K.: JSOT Press, 1987).

[8]Nicholas Wolterstorff's comment that Jesus blessed the poor, but not their condition of poverty, requires much more thorough grounding in these New Testament texts. See *Until Justice and Peace Embrace* (Grand Rapids, Mich.: Eerdmans, 1983), pp. 76-77.

[9]Richard Horsely, *Jesus and the Spiral of Violence* (San Francisco: Harper & Row, 1987), p. 78.

[10]Ibid.

[11]Ibid., p. 179.

[12]W. Pilgrim, *Good News to the Poor* (Minneapolis: Augsburg, 1981), p. 124.

[13]Johnson, *Sharing Possessions*, p. 77.

[14]So also Pilgrim, *Good News*, p. 129.

[15]Horsely, like those who witnessed the event, is so stunned by the unlikelihood that he, with the modern critical spirit of scientific erasure, has decided that the tradition claiming that Jesus was a friend of "publicans [tax collectors] and sinners" must have been fabricated. His reasoning is grounded in the premise that Christ, because of his orientation toward the revolutionary movements of his day, would not have befriended collaborators with the evil Roman system. I would rather doubt this premise than the clear testimony of the Gospels. Indeed, I see no compelling reason to accept it. Horsely, *Spiral of Violence*, p. 212.

[16]Wolterstorff, *Until Justice and Peace Embrace*, p. 3.

[17]H. Schürmann, *Das Lukasevangelium* (Freiberg, Germany: Herder, 1969), p. 498.

[18]Gordon writes of this text, "It is difficult to gauge the import of this change of instructions, but it could mean in the era to come, when Jesus is not with them as he has been, the apostles must take a radically different attitude to possessions than the one which was appropriate for their sojourn with him" (*Economic Problem*, p. 67).

[19]Pilgrim, too, seems correct in his view that the command to surrender everything in

the more literal and separatistically radical way did not endure beyond Jesus' death. Pilgrim, *Good News,* and discussion of alternative views, pp. 101-2.

Chapter 8: Four Parables About the Rich & Their Riches

[1]Jacques Ellul, *Money and Power,* trans. LaVonne Neff (Downers Grove, Ill.: InterVarsity Press, 1984), p. 138. Thomas E. Schmidt makes a similarly sweeping statement: "Every time Jesus offers an opinion about riches, it is negative. Every time he teaches about the use of wealth, he counsels his disciples to give it away" ("The Hard Sayings of Jesus," in *The Midas Trap,* ed. David Neff [Wheaton, Ill.: Scripture Press/Victor Books, 1990], p. 21).

[2]Ronald J. Sider, *Rich Christians in an Age of Hunger,* rev. ed. (Dallas: Word, 1990), pp. 109-10.

[3]Ibid., p. 110. Here I pass over the assertion that such things as "faster transportation . . . do not enrich our lives." Presumably Sider drives a car rather than a horse and buggy because he believes (rightly) that the faster mode of transportation enriches his life in all sorts of ways. And even if he did opt for slower means, by what standard (besides mere personal preference) would he confidently make such sweeping, accusatory judgments of people? Let us remember that we are discussing *God's* judgment of human beings. Our standards must pretty clearly not be those of mere personal taste (or distaste) for one style of life or another. And our words should be few.

[4]See the commentary on this by I. Howard Marshall, *Commentary on Luke,* New International Greek Testament Commentary (Grand Rapids, Mich.: Eerdmans, 1978), p. 521.

[5]Commentator Norval Geldenhuis agrees that "in this parable and these pronouncements the Saviour does not condemn the possession of worldly goods as such, but . . . the covetousness and carnal attitude with regard to earthly wealth" (*Commentary on the Gospel of Luke,* New International Commentary on the New Testament [1951; reprint Grand Rapids, Mich.: Eerdmans, 1975], p. 355).

[6]Again, for critical commentary I recommend Marshall, *Commentary on Luke,* pp. 613-26.

[7]See references in W. Pilgrim, *Good News to the Poor* (Minneapolis: Augsburg, 1981), p. 116, n. 25. In my interpretation, the distressing existence of hell, or some intermediate zone between heaven and hades, must be taken quite seriously in view of Jesus' warnings that follow about eternal life. As to the literal description and many other nuances of interpretation, see Marshall, *Commentary on Luke,* pp. 636-37.

[8]I do not wish to exclude God's freedom to extend his grace, in the kingdom of God, to people whose lives have been, in whatever respect, truly wretched so that in his kindness, and for reasons known only to him, he decides in his good will to include them. The text gives us no grounds for asserting, as Brian Griffiths does, that "Lazarus was a man of faith" (*The Creation of Wealth* [Downers Grove, Ill.: InterVarsity Press, 1985], p. 46). All we know is that Lazarus was a man of most wretched misery. And it is certainly not outside the realm of possibility that God's final judgment will constitute mercy for people whose lives have been nothing but wretched in this world.

What I reject is the claim that just being poor is either a necessary or a sufficient condition for receiving salvation. Neither is being rich a necessary or sufficient condition for being excluded. Marshall's carefully argued point seems to me obviously true of the parable: "It is quite false to infer that the rich man's lack of charity does not figure in the story" *(Commentary on Luke,* p. 636).

[9]On the name of Lazarus—a play on Abraham's servant by the same name, or on the miracle of Jesus' raising the real Lazarus—see Marshall, *Commentary on Luke,* p. 635. The name means literally "he whom God helps."

[10]I believe a comprehensive study of the New Testament from this perspective would support my claim about "nearness" in this parable. It certainly applies to the intense particularity and lack of typical political consciousness in the works of Jesus.

[11]Pilgrim is correct that "this unique Lukan parable demonstrates in a striking way Luke's concern for *the right use of possessions" (Good News,* p. 125; italics mine). Marshall appears to agree: *Commentary on Luke,* p. 622.

[12]Pilgrim, *Good News,* p. 126 and n. 5.; also Marshall, *Commentary on Luke,* pp. 614-15.

[13]In my view, then, this "appendage" is not at all "awkward," as Luke Johnson (expressing the view of many New Testament scholars) says that it is: *Sharing Possessions: Mandate and Symbol of Faith* (Philadelphia: Fortress, 1981), p. 17. My sense is that the flow from the parable to the sayings about mammon is quite reasonable and effective in bringing out the various points among Jesus' teachings on the subject in Luke's Gospel.

[14]In view of its great strategic importance to the unfolding vision of economic life in the New Testament, it is quite extraordinary that influential books by recent liberation theologians neglect it. This omission glares at us in two very influential essays. No discussion of the parable occurs in either Sider, *Rich Christians,* or Gustavo Gutiérrez, *A Theology of Liberation: History, Politics and Salvation,* trans. and ed. Caridad Inda and John Eagleson (Maryknoll, N.Y.: Orbis, 1973).

[15]The parable also expands and confirms the interpretation in my previous chapter on Zacchaeus's transformation and its significance as a paradigm for Christians living after Jesus' departure.

[16]There are differences between this parable of the ten pounds and Matthew's parable of the talents (Mt 25:14-30). Matthew has only three servants, whereas Luke has ten. Matthew's servants each receive a *large* sum of money for investment, whereas Luke's receive only about three months' wages. For a fuller discussion the reader may wish to consult Marshall, *Commentary on Luke,* p. 700.

[17]Johnson rightly notes the connection between the language of this parable and that of the parable of the dishonest manager. The theology of both stories is not the evils of wealth but "that the followers of Jesus are expected to *use* their possessions in a creative way" *(Sharing Possessions,* p. 18).

[18]Marshall suggests that the servant's statement "You take out what you did not put in and reap what you did not sow" suggests that the servant thought that even were he to make money, the nobleman would take it from him. See his *Commentary on Luke,* pp. 706-7. However, the master's response that the servant could have put the pound

in a bank indicates something to the effect that a safer way of enlarging the money would have been possible.

[19]As Griffiths states, "It is difficult not to broaden the lesson of the parable so that its meaning extends to all the resources which we have been given" *(Creation of Wealth,* p. 48).

Chapter 9: Lifestyles of the Rich & Faithful in the Early Church

[1]On the nature of ancient narrative, see G. B. Caird, *The Language and Imagery of the Bible* (Philadelphia: Westminster Press, 1980), especially pp. 201-18. On Luke's commitment to reliable history, see F. F. Bruce, *The Book of Acts,* New International Commentary on the New Testament (Grand Rapids, Mich.: Eerdmans, 1973), pp. 15-24.

[2]Barry Gordon, *The Economic Problem in Biblical and Patristic Thought* (Leiden, Netherlands: Brill, 1989), p. 79.

[3]Art Gish, "Decentralist Economics," in *Wealth and Poverty: Four Christian Views,* ed. Robert Clouse (Downers Grove, Ill.: InterVarsity Press, 1984), p. 139. Also Gordon, *Economic Problem,* p. 79.

[4]Gish, "Decentralist Economics," p. 144. The moral evils of capitalism are in its "primary moral commitments" of profit and growth and in that "private property, egoism, competition, materialism and greed are promoted."

[5]As an alternative, Gish promotes his New Covenant Fellowship, which is a communal vegetable farm using "a minimum of machinery, most of the work being done by hand," and a kind of poverty based in "the logic of the Incarnation" that leads to "simple living" (ibid., p. 151). Others agree, although often they favor state-controlled economies rather than the countercultural model of separate communal units—for instance, John Gladwin, as noted earlier in "Centralist Economics," in *Wealth and Poverty,* pp. 181-97.

[6]See Gordon, *Economic Problem,* pp. 78-79 and especially p. 81: "In any event it is clear that the Jerusalem case was a unique one." Also, J. A. Ziesler is among those who believe that the Jerusalem strategy was a display of gross financial imcompetence that caused the later impoverishment of the Jerusalem church. See Ziesler, *Christian Asceticism* (Grand Rapids, Mich.: Eerdmans, 1973), p. 110; and Wayne Meeks, *The First Urban Christians: The Social World of the Apostle Paul* (New Haven, Conn.: Yale University Press, 1983). These works provide important correctives to the impression given by Justo Gonzalez that the Jerusalem example was deeply influential in the early patristic church; see *Faith and Wealth* (San Francisco: Harper & Row, 1990).

Reconstructionist David Chilton also believes that the Jerusalem strategy was a one-time experiment, but his explanation, that it was a burst of charity for alien Jews who had come as pilgrims for Pentecost and ran short of funds, seems implausible. See Chilton, *Productive Christians in an Age of Guilt Manipulators* (Tyler, Tex.: Institute for Christian Economics, 1981), pp. 168-69. Being an unnatural reading of the text, this explanation requires that we believe that Jewish people sold *lands and houses,* thus divesting themselves of their most precious assets, just to perform a single, short-lived act of goodwill toward fellow Jews. Chilton adds that real estate had become a poor investment anyway, because the Romans were on the move. But he gives no solid social and historical evidence to show that the Roman presence had this psychological effect in other areas of the market. To my knowledge, there is no such evidence. Sider is quite right in citing famine as the main cause of poverty there *(Rich Christians,* pp. 91-92, and references).

[7]See Bruce, *Book of Acts,* p. 110.

[8]Jouette Bassler, like many biblical scholars, is quick to detect conflicts in the narrative. She judges that these statements (in Acts 4) unexpectedly and suddenly contradict those made about having "all things in common" (in Acts 2). "It is also surprising to find the general summaries so quickly contradicted" *(God and Mammon: Asking for Money in the New Testament* [Nashville: Abingdon, 1991], p. 126). However, I see no reason to indict Luke of what amounts to considerable weak-mindedness on this point. Why not rather conclude that Luke gave important nuances in Acts 4 to the accounts in Acts 2? This seems the more sympathetic and reasonable approach.

[9]Bruce, *Book of Acts,* p. 113.

[10]Sider, *Rich Christians,* p. 90.

[11]W. Pilgrim writes: "What Luke has in mind is not a total selling of all one's possessions at one time and then living off the proceeds from that moment on, but a continual selling and sharing as the needs emerged or as the treasury became low" *(Good News for the Poor* [Minneapolis: Augsburg, 1981], p. 151).

[12]See Nicholas Wolterstorff and Alvin Plantinga, eds., *Faith and Rationality: Reason and Belief in God* (Notre Dame, Ind.: University of Notre Dame Press, 1983).

[13]Cited in Gustavo Gutiérrez, *A Theology of Liberation: History, Politics and Salvation,* trans. and ed. Caridad Inda and John Eagleson (Maryknoll, N.Y.: Orbis, 1973), p. 301.

[14]For a forceful development of this protest see Michael Novak, *Will It Liberate? Questions About Liberation Theology* (New York: Paulist, 1986).

[15]Sider, *Rich Christians,* p. 164.

[16]Ibid. Liberation theologians agree that the poverty of the Christian is grounded in both the imitation of Christ and the book of Acts. See Gutiérrez, *Theology of Liberation,* pp. 300-302.

[17]I pass over the inconsistency here in affirming productive capital while negating the forms of investment security and consumption of the superfluous, which make successful capitalistic systems possible.

[18]See Pamela D. Couture, *Blessed Are the Poor?* (Nashville: Abingdon, 1991), on Wesley, pp. 119-34.

[19]If I understand Couture's thesis correctly, it is implicitly an attack on what I have called "nearness." She calls it "family idolatry" and recommends instead an ethic of "indifference." In translation, this means that "poor people are poor people," no matter how we are related to them in time, space or intimacy. In consistent practice, it thus seems headed for the whole desperate and joyless psychology of unlimited obligations. She adds to this (quite logically) the typically contemporary diminishment of the *family* as a primary context for human flourishing.

[20]Sider, *Rich Christians*, p. 90.

[21]See Gordon, *Economic Problem*, pp. 59-60, for his own view and supporting references to that of others.

[22]Ibid., p. 60.

[23]See Bassler, *God and Mammon*, p. 89. It is somewhat odd that Luke fails to mention the poverty of the Jerusalem church and Paul's collection of welfare from the richer congregations around the Empire; on this see Gordon, *Economic Problem*, p. 78.

[24]Acts 15 and Galatians 2 recount how the agreement to perform such duties was struck at the Jerusalem Council of A.D. 48. Paul writes of it in 2 Corinthians 8 and 9, as well as in Romans 15.

[25]For instance, Sider believes that Paul offers in these passages a general biblical definition of "economic koinonia." By this Sider means that Paul required that all Christian "fellowship" include economic relationships patterned after the models that he gave to the Corinthian church. Sider, *Rich Christians*, p. 92.

[26]Ibid., p. 96.

[27]Ibid.

[28]Ibid., p. 98.

[29]Bassler, *God and Mammon*, pp. 94-96.; see also Luke Johnson, *Sharing Possessions: Mandate and Symbol of Faith* (Philadelphia: Fortress, 1981), pp. 112-13.

[30]Bassler, *God and Mammon*, pp. 94-95.

[31]Johnson, *Sharing Possessions*, p. 112.

[32]Ibid.

[33]Elsewhere Paul writes harshly of Christians who have left work and responsibilities to go on romantic quests. See, for example, 1 Corinthians 7:24; 2 Thessalonians 2:1-12. And Gordon's observation is correct: "The epistles of Paul do not display the degree of tension evident in Luke concerning ownership of capital, economic status and discipleship" (*Economic Problem*, p. 70).

[34]Gordon's judgment about Paul seems right: "It is impossible to detect any trace of such an affiliation [with asceticism or divestment] in Paul, who puts no great store on systematic voluntary restriction of consumption, or an abandonment of personal capital" (*Economic Problem*, p. 62).

For Further Reading

Augustine. *The City of God.* Abridged and edited by V. Bourke. Translated by G. Walsh, Demetrius B. Zema, Grace Monahan and Daniel Honan. Garden City, N.Y.: Doubleday/Image Books, 1958.

The Babylonian Genesis. Translated and edited by Alexander Heidel. 2d ed. Chicago: University of Chicago Press, 1963.

Bassler, Jouette. *God and Mammon: Asking for Money in the New Testament.* Nashville: Abingdon, 1991.

Batey, Richard A. *Jesus and the Forgotten City.* Grand Rapids, Mich.: Baker Book House, 1992.

Bellah, Robert, et al. *Habits of the Heart: Individualism and Commitment in American Life.* New York: Harper & Row, 1985.

Boorstin, Daniel. *The Lost World of Thomas Jefferson.* 1948; reprint Chicago: University of Chicago Press, 1981.

Calvin, John. *Institutes of the Christian Religion.* Edited by John T. McNeill. Translated by Ford Lewis Battles. Library of Christian Classics 20. Philadelphia: Westminster Press, 1967.

Chilton, David. *Productive Christians in an Age of Guilt Manipulators.* Tyler, Tex.: Institute for Christian Economics, 1981.

Cooper, John. *Body, Soul and Life Everlasting.* Grand Rapids, Mich.: Eerdmans, 1989.

Couture, Pamela D. *Blessed Are the Poor?* Nashville: Abingdon, 1991.

DeVos, Richard. *Compassionate Capitalism: People Helping People Help Themselves.* New York: Dutton, 1993.

Ellis, M., and O. Maduro, eds. *The Future of Liberation Theology: Essays in Honor of Gustavo Gutierrez.* Maryknoll, N.Y.: Orbis, 1989.

Ellul, Jacques. *Money and Power.* Translated by LaVonne Neff. Downers Grove: Inter-

Varsity Press, 1984.

Frankfort, Henri. *The Intellectual Adventure of Ancient Man.* Chicago: University of Chicago Press, 1977.

Gladwin, John. "Centralist Economics." In *Wealth and Poverty: Four Christian Views,* edited by R. Clouse. Downers Grove, Ill.: InterVarsity Press, 1984.

Gonzalez, Justo. *Faith and Wealth.* San Francisco: Harper, 1990.

————. *The Story of Christianity.* San Francisco: Harper & Row, 1984.

Gordon, Barry. *The Economic Problem in Biblical and Patristic Thought.* Leiden, Netherlands: Brill, 1989.

Green, Robert, ed. *Protestantism and Capitalism: The Weber Thesis and Its Critics.* Boston: Heath, 1959.

Griffiths, Brian, *The Creation of Wealth.* Downers Grove, Ill.: InterVarsity Press, 1985.

Hardy, Lee. *The Fabric of This World.* Grand Rapids, Mich.: Eerdmans, 1991.

Hengel, Martin. *Property and Riches in the Early Church.* Translated by John Bowden. Ann Arbor, Mich.: University Microfilms/Books on Demand, n.d.

Holmberg, B. *Sociology and the New Testament: An Appraisal.* Minneapolis: Augsburg/Fortress, 1990.

Horsely, Richard. *Jesus and the Spiral of Violence.* San Francisco: Harper & Row, 1987.

Horsely, Richard, and J. S. Hanson. *Bandits, Prophets and Messiahs: Popular Movements at the Time of Jesus.* San Francisco: Harper & Row, 1985.

John Paul II. *Laborem Exercens: On Human Work.* Sydney, Australia: St. Paul, 1981.

Johnson, Luke T. *Sharing Possessions: Mandate and Symbol of Faith.* Philadelphia: Fortress, 1981.

Lilburne, Geoffrey R. *A Sense of Place: A Christian Theology of the Land.* Nashville: Abingdon, 1989.

Limburg, James. *The Prophets and the Powerless.* Atlanta: John Knox Press, 1977.

Luther, Martin. "An Appeal to the Ruling Class." In *Martin Luther,* edited and translated by John Dillenberger. Garden City, N.Y.: Doubleday/Anchor Books, 1961.

Meeks, Wayne. *The First Urban Christians: The Social World of the Apostle Paul.* New Haven, Conn.: Yale University Press, 1983.

Mott, Stephen. *Biblical Ethics and Social Change.* New York: Oxford University Press, 1982.

Mouw, Richard. *Political Evangelism.* Grand Rapids, Mich.: Eerdmans, 1973.

Neff, David, ed. *The Midas Trap.* Wheaton, Ill.: Scripture Press/Victor Books, 1990.

Neuhaus, Richard John. *Doing Well and Doing Good.* New York: Doubleday, 1992.

Niebuhr, H. Richard. *Christ and Culture.* New York: Harper & Row/Harper Torch Books, 1951.

North, Robert. *The Sociology of the Biblical Jubilee.* Rome: Pontifical Biblical Institute, 1954.

Novak, Michael. *The Spirit of Democratic Capitalism.* Lanham, Md.: University Press of America/Madison Books, 1991.

————. *Will It Liberate? Questions About Liberation Theology.* New York: Paulist, 1986.

Oakman, Douglas. *Jesus and the Economic Question of His Day.* Lewiston, N.Y.: Edwin Mellen, 1986.

Pilgrim, W. *Good News to the Poor.* Minneapolis: Augsburg, 1981.

Safrai, S., et al., eds. *The Jewish People in the First Century: Historical Geography, Political History, Social, Cultural and Religious Life and Institutions.* Vol. 2. Philadelphia: Fortress, 1987.

Schmidt, Thomas E. *Hostility to Wealth in the Synoptic Gospels.* Sheffield, U.K.: JSOT, 1987.

Stambaugh, John, and David Balch. *The Social World of the First Christians.* London: SPCK, 1986.

Theissen, Gerd. *Sociology of Early Palestinian Christianity.* Philadelphia: Fortress, 1977.

Toward the Future: Catholic Social Thought and the U.S. Economy—A Lay Letter by the Lay Commission on Catholic Social Thinking. American Catholic Committee, 1984.

White, Lynn, Jr. "The Historical Roots of our Ecological Crisis." *Science,* March 10, 1967.

Wolterstorff, Nicholas. *Until Justice and Peace Embrace.* Grand Rapids, Mich.: Eerdmans, 1983.

Ziesler, J. A. *Christian Asceticism.* Grand Rapids, Mich.: Eerdmans, 1973.

Index of Names

Index of Scripture